SEVEN STYLES
of
PARENTING

SEVEN STYLES
of
PARENTING

by
PAT HERSHEY OWEN

Tyndale House
Publishers, Inc.
Wheaton, Illinois

First printing, trade paper edition, September 1984
Library of Congress Catalog Card Number 83-50276
ISBN 0-8423-5873-0, paper
Copyright © 1983 by Pat Hershey Owen
Printed in the United States of America

With a heart
full of thanksgiving
I gratefully dedicate
this book
to the Giver of gifts . . .
the precious
Holy Spirit

CONTENTS

FOREWORD

"Our knowledge is always incomplete and our prophecy is always incomplete, and when the complete comes, that is the end of the incomplete.

"At present we are men looking at puzzling reflections in a mirror. The time will come when we shall see reality whole and face to face! At present all I know is a little fraction of the truth, but the time will come when I shall know it as fully as God has known me!" (1 Corinthians 13:9, 10, 12, Phillips).

Within the writings of the Talmud it is written, "As a hammer splits the rock into many splinters, so will a scriptural verse yield many meanings."

This book is offered as one of the many splinters from the portions of Scripture that speak of God's gifts. It is offered as an aid to help parents better understand themselves, their children, and each other—as well as to tap the measureless wisdom of our loving God, who longs to draw us into oneness with himself.

—*Pat Hershey Owen*

ONE

PARENTING AND PERSONAL GIFTS

Boyish excitement was written all over Phil's face as he slammed the car door and bounded up the front steps three at a time. He burst into the house, tossed his attaché case onto a sofa, and strode through the dining room into the kitchen, where his wife was bent over the cutting board.

He grabbed her and swung her around a couple of times, then set her down in the middle of the floor. He straddled a kitchen chair and grinned impishly at his wife.

"What's got into you, Phil?" she asked, smoothing her dress.

"I thought you'd want to know," he said. "Watch this." Slowly and dramatically he slid his wallet from his pocket. He opened it and began pulling out twenty-dollar bills, one at a time, and fanning them out on the kitchen table.

"Phil . . . where did you get all that . . . ?"

"I got my raise," Phil grinned. "*And* a bonus. A good one. Retroactive."

"That's wonderful," Cathy said. "I'm proud of you. . . ."

"Now I can give you that vacation you've been needing . . . we can go to that quaint little village north of San Francisco . . . two whole weeks, beginning on Monday. Just think, Cathy. . ." In his excitement Phil began to pace back and forth.

"Just think . . . no cooking. No housekeeping . . . just resting. Reading. The things you'd like to do." He scooped up the pile of bills and thrust them into her hands. "Take them. It's all yours to spend. And there's more. I'm going to give some to our pastor, so he can take his wife on a vacation, too."

Cathy stood with her hands full of the twenty-dollar bills, a slight frown on her face. She was standing like that when Sara skipped into the room.

"Hi, Dad. You're home early. Hi, Mom. . . ." She paused and her mouth dropped open. "Money! Mother, where did you get all that?"

"What's all the commotion?" came Andy's voice from the doorway. "I could hear you before I got in the house!"

Phil turned to his children. "I got a raise. And a bonus. So we're going to give Mother a restful vacation. On the coast above San Francisco. You know the place. And. . . ."

Sara clapped her hands. "That's wonderful. That's near the North Shore Mission. Remember, the one the missionary speaker told us about a couple of weeks ago? I can't forget all of those needy people in the area . . . and how the mission needs help. We could spend most of our days at the mission helping. . . ."

Andy interrupted, "North of San Francisco! That's the route Father Junipero Serra took. I've been reading about him. I even checked out several library books just today to learn about how he founded that string of California missions. Sara, since you're so gung-ho on missions, why don't you go read this book? And Dad, here's one for you and Mother to bone up on. It's all about the history of the whole area."

PARENTING AND PERSONAL GIFTS

"Wait a minute," Phil said. "Andy, I'm not talking about an educational seminar. And Sara, your mother doesn't need to spend two weeks working somewhere."

"Be quiet, all of you," Cathy said as she carefully laid the sheaf of bills on the counter. "There are many things to consider. We can't just go."

"But why not?" Phil asked. "You've earned it. We've even talked about it." He looked disappointed.

"But, Mother," Sara wailed, "that mission needs us. . . ."

"And it'll be useful to study these books . . . anyway, I've already got them checked out," Andy said.

"I thought . . ." Phil started, the eagerness beginning to fade from his face. "I thought I could give you this time of rest and we'd all be happy about it. And that we'd just . . . just go . . ." he ended lamely.

Cathy shook her head. "Phil, we can't *just go*."

Phil stared out the window. "Of course not, we've got to consider laying out all the clothes in an *orderly* manner."

"Doesn't anybody care about the people at the mission?" Sara cried as she ran out of the room.

Nobody seemed to notice.

Most of us are familiar with family conferences like this, that begin so upbeat, and end with hurt feelings, misunderstandings, and even anger. And by the time it's all over with, nobody has the slightest idea what happened, except for the fact that everybody ended up edgy and upset.

How did it happen? But, even more importantly, *what* happened? Nobody wanted a family disagreement or argument. Everybody wanted only to be heard and understood. But it didn't turn out the way *anybody* wanted it to turn out.

Why was that?

That's a good question, and the answer is what this whole book is all about.

Many parents (in fact, if the truth were known, probably *most* parents) face perplexing dilemmas like the above. And if you had been involved in the above situation, depending upon your personal approach to parenting, you might have done one of several things:

(a) If you had been Phil, you might have slammed out of the house seeking someone who would appreciate your giving spirit.

(b) If you had been Cathy you might have discouragingly wondered why your family always seemed to see only their own interests, and not the big picture and how it affected everyone.

(c) If you had been Andy, you might have thought your family was not as intellectual as you because the others were not as interested in an educational approach.

(d) Or, if you had been Sara, you might have concluded that the other family members weren't very "spiritual" because they didn't seem at all interested in the plight of the mission people.

All of the above leads us to the question: As a parent, what is your personal approach? Is it a "giving" approach—as was Phil's to his family? Is it an "organizational" approach—as was Cathy's? Or an educational "teaching" approach—as was Andy's? A "merciful" approach—as was Sara's? Or, is it something different from any of the above?

Each parent can identify one of seven styles or manners which describe his own approach (four of which are touched on in the above illustration). We approach parenting as we are directed, led, or impelled by our God-given "personal gift." The Bible says that God has given one of these personal gifts to everyone. Personally, I believe that one of these gifts (which are actually the quintessence of our personalities) has been given to every child at birth.

This fact will help explain the oft-heard remark made by many frustrated parents, "My children are all so different! I can understand John because he's like his father. And I can understand Beth because she's like me. But I don't understand Joan at all. She is not like any of the rest of the family!"

The answer to this seemingly perplexing problem may lie wrapped up in the understanding of our personal gifts. And in the case of the situation above, Joan might just have a different personal gift than the other members of the family.

By now you are probably asking, "Just what are these personal gifts?" The answer to this seeming mystery is to be found in the book of Romans where verse 6 of chapter 12 begins, "Having then gifts . . . ," followed by a list of the seven different *charismata* or personal gifts: prophecy, ministry, teaching, exhorting, giving, ruling, and mercy.

Because the root of the Greek word, *chara,* means joy or gladness, the seven gifts named in these verses are to be considered as "gifts of joy." So when a man, woman, boy, or girl uses his gift, the awareness of that gift and the use of it brings true joy and gladness.

These joyous gifts of grace are special to each recipient. They are vital to every person, especially to each child of God. And since they come from God as gifts freely bestowed, they are not externally imposed. They come from within.

The importance of this statement cannot be overemphasized: since God has already given me one of these personal gifts, I don't have to try, strain, or strive to possess one of them. I already possess one. It's a gift that's already been given. He gave it to me, and it's mine. The parameters of that personal gift define or determine the manner in which I approach any situation, task, involvement, or opportunity of service.

For example, my own personal gift is *ruling,* which means that I *approach* all of my family, business, and church situations in the same manner. Basically, this means that I have the ability to see the overall picture in just about any project I am confronted with or a part of. I have the ability to organize people and projects so that the task can be accomplished in the most efficient manner possible, even delegating some or much to be done in order to set and attain completion goals.

This approach isn't something I consciously consider. It's an intrinsic part of me. And in the exercise of that approach I experience a "comfortableness," a joy that bubbles up from the very depths of me. This *charisma,* this personal gift of ruling (or administration, as it is called in some translations) is, to me, definitely a gracious gift of joy.

On the other hand, my husband's personal gift is mercy. So, in any given situation, the two of us approach a solution differently. My approach is not always the best; nor is his approach always the best. In most cases, they are just different.

Even as I approach situations in the administrative mode, Bob approaches every situation in the mercy mode. For him this means that his actions are characterized by a desire and capacity to remove hurts and to bring healing to others. He actually identifies with those who are hurting or in distress, whether it be physical or emotional. And, since he has a strong desire to promote harmony and to work for peace, you can see that our approaches might in some cases *seem to be working at cross purposes* with each other.

Now, for an example. My husband and I are both writers and often assist each other on our writing projects. And since we still have children living at home, this means that I also have many household chores to oversee, in addition to my stints at my typewriter. Bob is very considerate of me and of the extra duties that are mine, so he frequently helps me with my work.

Conversely, when Bob's writing schedules are such that he is facing a pressured completion date on some project, I will drop everything and help him.

One such writing project was imposing heavy demands upon Bob's time and energies. In the midst of it, with only days to go to finish an assigned book, both of us were bending practically all of our energies, from early morning till late at night, to meet our contract date.

At this crucial time, a family with whom we were slightly acquainted began to experience some marital difficulties, and because of the emotional trauma, the wife was hospitalized. Bob (in his approach of mercy) stopped writing in the middle of a page and went to the hospital.

I objected. "Bob, there is really nothing you can do for them.

At least nothing that you can do right at this minute. Let's get this job done first."

Bob looked ruefully at his typewriter and the unfinished stack of pages. "You may be right, Pat," he said, "but this could be a crucial time for them. . . ."

"It *could be* a crucial time for them," I countered. "But *it is* a crucial time for us. We've got less than a week to complete all this. . . ." I waved my hand at the stack, groaning inwardly at the thought of the long hours at our typewriters that still remained.

He hesitated. "Pat, I'm sorry, but they need me. I'll be back as soon as I can."

It was even as he was backing out of our driveway that the thought came to me: *This is an exact illustration of what we are writing about.* Though Bob knew his taking leave of his typewriter for a few hours would impose even heavier demands upon both of us, his *mercy approach* to Jim and Rita's problem caused him to see their need and act according to his innate desire to promote healing.

And even though he would now have to work longer and harder to complete his project on time, Bob attended to Jim and Rita with great joy. I thank God that his love enabled me to be gracious to Bob when he returned to his typewriter.

As I analyzed what he had done, I could see that Bob's gift of mercy had impelled him to minister immediately to Jim and Rita's hurts. Though at times these traits of his have caused me some personal inconvenience, I realize he is the most fulfilled when he acts and moves as his gift of mercy directs, even as I am the most fulfilled when I act and move as my gift of ruling directs.

By the illustration you can see the difference between the way my husband and I approach situations: entirely differently. Mine is usually geared to the most logical, straightforward, quickest, most efficient manner of doing anything—often (perhaps even usually) delegating tasks in order to achieve my goals and/or purposes.

Bob's compassionate nature, on the other hand, will usually

compel him to become personally involved in the hurting needs of others around him.

So you can see, it isn't that we desire to think differently or to act differently. We just *do* think and act differently. Nor is it a matter of spiritual maturity or putting God first. Spiritual maturity is not determined by one's approach to a situation. Spiritual maturity is determined by consistent obedience to God. Psalm 119:1 defines this very well. The ones who consistently obey God are called the "undefiled—the upright, truly sincere and blameless—in the way [of the revealed will of God]; who walk—that is, order their conduct and conversation—in (the whole of God's revealed will) the law of the Lord" *(The Amplified Bible).*

An excellent example of the above can be illustrated by the leadership of two outstanding men of God, each with a different *charisma* (personal gift), but each filling the same position at different times. Dr. Bob Pierce was the founder and first president of World Vision, an organization that has cared for hundreds of thousands of homeless and needy children.

"Dr. Bob," as he was called, was in Korea during the Korean conflict, when he first became aware of the staggering numbers of children that were orphaned by the hostilities. His merciful nature directed him to empty his pockets to provide for one of them.

Though he had cared for one, there were other thousands who were eking out a bare existence on the streets. Bob returned to the States and began raising money to care for the orphans. The organization now known as World Vision was the result. Dr. Bob's approach to everything he did was directed by his personal gift of mercy—even his administration of the infant organization.

Today, World Vision, International, is a multimillion-dollar, multifaceted Christian relief agency, headed by Dr. Ted Engstrom, whose personal gift is ruling (administration). Whereas Dr. Bob's personal gift of mercy impelled him to reach out in love to that first World Vision child, Dr. Engstrom's personal gift of ruling (administration) has enabled him to plan, organize, and delegate responsibilities to other gifted men and women in such a way as to greatly broaden the scope and depth of World Vision's expanding vision for the world's needy.

However, it must be understood that neither man was necessarily more spiritually mature than the other; both men were equally used of God in the same position at different times. And both of them, by approaching their tasks as directed by their particular personal gift, did so with great joy.

So you can see that when two or more people approach a given situation differently *(because each possesses a different personal gift),* as long as each is responding to God according to his revealed Word, that person is right in his or her approach.

A principle to remember at this point is: When two people with different personal gifts view the work (or actions, or ministries) of others, they *tend to evaluate others from the viewpoint of their own personal gift.* Which means that unless one possesses a solid understanding of all seven of the personal gifts, he could and very likely would become impatient with people who have personal gifts different from his own.

The illustration given at the beginning of this chapter is an excellent example of the above. Sara believed that none of the other family members were as "spiritual" as she, because none responded to the needs of the mission. This was not necessarily true, but Sara believed it to be true, because she was evaluating every one from her viewpoint of the personal gift of mercy—even as Andy was evaluating the family from his personal gift of teaching; Cathy was evaluating from her personal gift of ruling (administration); and Phil was evaluating from his personal gift of giving. So strife developed in the home because none clearly understood either his own personal gift or the gifts of others.

By knowing our own personal gift—and being able to define the personal gifts of our children—we will learn how to avoid frustrating family scenes such as the one portrayed at the beginning of this chapter.

We will also learn the dangers of perverting, submerging, or sublimating our personal gifts. We will learn how to operate within the parameters of our gift, with great joy. This fact will become more and more evident as we proceed, for I will be defining, clarifying, and instructing you—as a parent—in how to utilize your own personal gift so that you will be more able to "parent" with joy.

At the same time, you will then be able yourself to define and clarify your children's gifts. By so doing, you will have taken a quantum leap into the position of being able to minimize and/or eliminate the irritations that occasionally crop up in any home between parents and children, between siblings, and even between parents themselves.

And that's really a reason to praise the Lord!

Let me outline briefly some of the principles you will be discovering within the next few pages, and on to the conclusion of this book:

First, since there are seven types of gifts, there will, of necessity, be seven approaches to parenting. When this becomes crystal clear in your thinking, then you won't mind the fact that you and your spouse might possess different personal gifts. Then you will begin to understand why he acts as he does in a given situation, while you act in an entirely different manner. You will then be enabled to understand that these different approaches to parenting (or any other life situation) are not the result of different levels of spirituality at all, but are God-implanted approaches or responses that are natural to the possessors of the seven different *charismata* or personal gifts.

So as you become fully aware of these seven gifts and how they have an impact or operate in each person, especially each parent, you will more patiently accept the differences between the actions of yourself and your mate, yourself and your individual children, and between the children themselves.

Second, this also means that, again, since there are seven personal gifts possessed by children as well as adults, that there are seven different manners or styles in which children will approach any life situation. Again, this information will take the pressure off, so to speak, when you observe the fact that your children respond differently to the same stimuli, situations, and even people. And when you know this, and get a good grasp of how these seven gifts are evidenced in different children, then the entire atmosphere of your home will improve.

The reason being: you are no longer desirous of forcing any member of the household—either mate or child—into one mold. You will, instead, learn which of the personal gifts is resident in each member of your family, then respond to each accordingly. You will learn to harmonize your approach with the six other approaches. In the Hebrew language, the number seven always carries with it the connotation of perfection or completeness. I believe it is no accident that God gave these seven different *charismata* or personal gifts to his Body.

Romans, chapter 12, clearly indicates the vital interrelationship between the organs of our physical bodies as being analogous to the interrelationships of the members of his Body, the church. "Just as there are many parts to our bodies," Paul is telling us in verses 4, 5, *The Living Bible,* "so it is with Christ's body. We are all parts of it, and it takes everyone of us to make it complete . . . and each needs all the others."

Every believer is urged "not to think of himself (or his personal gift) more highly than he ought to think" (Romans 12:3); this is essential, in fact, crucial to the smooth-working of Christ's Body. Each of us is needed—regardless of the personal gift we possess—in order to make the Body of Christ complete. This is what God intended.

With this foundational background, I believe we are now ready to move into the next section of the book which covers in detail the *seven different styles (approaches)* of parenting.

THE PROPHECY STYLE OF PARENTING

Christmas was always a much-looked-forward-to event in our home when I was growing up. I remember how beautifully my mother always decorated our house, and how she brought much joy into my life with her singing. I especially remember a Christmas when I was in the fifth grade.

My cousin and uncle were going to spend the week with us. Sue was my age, and I remember that all she could talk about was the dollhouse she hoped she would be getting for Christmas. Dolls were all right, and I liked to play with them, too. But I was hoping to get something other than a doll this Christmas—like a racer sled, one that I could steer.

It was no wonder that we had so much difficulty getting to sleep Christmas Eve. Sue and I giggled and talked till late that night. And a couple of times my Uncle Milton came into the room to tell us to be quiet. We obeyed him, at least until he left the room. Then we covered our heads with the blankets and whispered.

"I so much hope I get that dollhouse . . ." were the last words I remember hearing that night. Then. . . .

"Merry Christmas, Patty! Merry Christmas, Sue! Time to get up!" It was my mother.

I sat up in bed and rubbed my eyes. Christmas! With a squeal, Sue and I both leaped out of bed and ran into the living room. The tree was sparkling with lights and ornaments. But neither of us had eyes for the tree. Our thoughts were upon something else.

Within moments, wrappings and gifts were scattered all around the room. And I was straddling my new sled: my racer. It would even steer! I had so longed for that sled. Now I could hardly wait to get outside into the snow and try it out.

Across the room from me was Sue with her dollhouse, with its rooms full of furniture! We were both noisily ecstatic.

My parents, and Uncle Milton, who was a pastor, were all pleased that we were so happy with our gifts. After breakfast they sat around and talked while we played. And played. It seemed that we could hardly get enough of playing with Sue's dollhouse. And my sled. That night we went to sleep quickly— happily exhausted from the day's activities.

The next morning it was Sunday, so we didn't have time to play before going to Sunday school. But as soon as we got home from church, Sue and I quickly changed our clothes and started again. We had her dollhouse set up in my bedroom and were having the best of times, when my Uncle Milton entered the room to call us to dinner.

Suddenly I was aware of his frown.

"Not on Sunday, Sue . . ." I heard him say.

Without another word, Sue began putting the dollhouse away. I couldn't understand. My parents made no restrictions on my Sunday playing, as long as I went to Sunday school and church. When Uncle Milton led Sue away crying, I was confused. Confused and angry.

I remember that Sue cried at the dinner table, while I sat and glared at my uncle. I hurriedly cleaned up my plate, excused myself, and went to my room to pout. Sue soon joined me there. But we had nothing to say. Our Sunday of playing was spoiled.

Then Uncle Milton came into the room. I started to glare at him again. But to my amazement, he was smiling. "I've got an idea," he began.

We just looked at him. Remembering how rigid Uncle Milton had always seemed, I couldn't imagine that he'd change his mind about the dollhouse. And I was right. But what he did say really surprised me.

"We just went to church," he was saying. "But the dolls *didn't* go to church. So let's pretend that we're taking the dolls to church—and we'll show the dolls how to act on Sunday. . . ."

In amazement I watched while my grown uncle began talking to Sue's dolls. "Remember, Jesus loves you," he said to one of the dolls. "And he wants you to be in church. . . ." Soon, despite my reluctance, I found myself, along with Sue, drawn into the project of "taking the dolls to church."

When we got the dolls to "church," Uncle Milton told us to seat them in a row, which we did. Then we taught choruses to the dolls, after which Uncle Milton "preached" to them (and to us). I didn't mind, though, because he didn't preach very long, and his sermon was about the Baby Jesus and the reasons why we celebrate Christmas. Then "church" was over and we could "go home."

"Now," I said, "let's go play with my new sled." Uncle Milton didn't frown this time, but he did shake his head. "Patty, instead of playing with your sled, which is something you can do *every day,* let's put it aside on the Lord's day."

I felt my anger rising again. But he went on. "Instead, let's the three of us go take a long walk in the snow and talk about the beautiful world that God has made for us to enjoy."

So we did. And, strangely enough, I admitted to myself later that it really did turn out to be a rather wonderful day. Though I had no way of knowing it then, I now realize that my Uncle Milton possessed the *charisma,* the personal gift of *prophecy.*

On that particular day, I thought (at first, anyway) that Uncle Milton had been rather dogmatic and unbending, because he expected me to conform to his will and his opinions. It seemed not to matter to him how we generally spent our Sundays; he expected us to fit in with his manner of living.

Understandably, I resented that. But even that seemed not to bother him. He was a man of principle, and it mattered not if others agreed with him. I have since come to respect these qualities in my Uncle Milton.

He is fearless in his presentation of the gospel message, whether he's preaching in the pulpit or sharing Jesus with a truck driver. And people listen to him. Some are repelled by his straightforward presentation of his views. Others love it. None can ignore either him or his message.

This fearlessness, this confidence and authority have enabled Uncle Milton to hew out several churches from nothing and build them into monuments of God's love. He has often gone door-to-door in new, strange communities "selling" people on their need for a church. Then he has—one by one—led many individuals in that community to make personal commitments to Jesus Christ.

He has resisted persecution, pain, and deprivation in order to build the kingdom of God. And he has done it successfully— *primarily because of his personal gift of prophecy.* He leads, he crusades, he wins. He refuses to be defeated.

For a while I thought Uncle Milton was and did all this *because he was a preacher.* But I have since learned that this is not so. For this gift—as is true with the other six personal gifts named in Romans 12:6-8—can be found evidenced in a wide spectrum of professions and occupations, and among people of all ages.

The gift of prophecy. What is it, anyway?

It is one of the *charismata,* personal gifts that are listed in Romans 12:6-8, which begins, "Having then gifts *[charismata]* ... whether prophecy...." In this context, the word "prophecy" is derived from the Greek word, *propheetia* and means to "speak out," to "declare." The word also carries with it the connotation of "proclaiming," especially in a forthright manner.

Doesn't this sound like my Uncle Milton?

The *charisma* (singular of the word) or personal gift of "prophecy," then, has to do with telling, declaring, proclaiming, speaking out. A person possessing the personal gift of prophecy is one who proclaims or speaks out. With such a person there is no wavering, no hesitation. He speaks the truth as he sees it, without hesitation. Whatever he believes is right, he acts on, regardless of the consequences.

The child of a parent with this gift will always have the confidence of knowing the stand or stance his parent has taken or will take. In spite of the parent's seeming harshness or inflexibility, the child can be assured that his father or mother will remain steady and always speak the same way: boldly, fearlessly, clearly, consistently. To put it another way, a parent possessing the personal gift of prophecy will exhibit a style of parenting that maintains the high profile of a person of action (tending often to make quick decisions), and standing for his views openly and single-mindedly. His zeal may be manifested in a persuasiveness, a competitiveness, or an aggressiveness. This parent is often dramatic and unorthodox in his teaching or discipline.

Let me further illustrate this personal gift of prophecy as I have seen it manifested in the lives of several people.

Dr. Weinheimer was the executive director of the Michigan Association of School Boards at the time I served the same organization as public relations director. Because of my strategic position, I was always aware of the pros and cons of every issue that affected the association. I was also aware that Dr. Weinheimer was a man who saw everything as black or white, and would not compromise on any issue for any reason, even for the sake of his own public image. No subject was too tough or controversial for him. It is interesting to note that Dr. W's approach to his important and highly visible public position was the identical approach he took in his role of father and grandfather. He was equally uncompromising to all his publics, including that of the school kids and their parents. When he took a position or stance he seemed impervious to what others thought or said.

Dr. W. loved to be in the middle of the action. And because his personal gift was that of prophecy, he felt a compulsion to express himself verbally. As a result, he developed his verbal skills until he became a master persuader. However, Dr. W's frankness was frequently interpreted by the press as harshness and unfeelingness. Yet those of us who knew him well knew this was not the case. It is true, however, that persons possessing the personal gift of prophecy do tend to avoid close personal contacts and intimacy, except in their most personal relationships. This characteristic, of course, may be and often is interpreted by others as aloofness or unfeelingness. This was so with Betty.

Betty had just returned from Central America where she had flown supplies to remote missionary villages. A family reception was given in her honor. In the midst of the festivities, the inevitable question came up.

"Betty, the work you do is dangerous, isn't it?" a man asked.

She smiled. "Yes, Frank, I suppose you could say so."

"Then why do you do it?"

All other conversation stopped and every ear was attuned to Betty's answer. "I guess the simplest answer is that I'm very good at jungle flying. I respond well to crisis situations—of which there are many. And . . . mostly, I find great joy in doing what I do just the way I do it."

A woman spoke. "There are many people who think it's wrong for a woman to be a jungle pilot. It seems so . . . so, well, unladylike."

Betty laughed pleasantly. "I really don't listen much to the opinions of others."

"But don't you ever get lonely? Aren't you ever afraid?"

"The answer to the first question is, seldom," Betty said. "To the second one, rarely. I know I am doing God's will. And I have his promise to go with me. So I go."

Typical of one with the personal gifts of prophecy, Betty has the remarkable ability to stand alone and persevere against all opposing forces.

Let me reiterate my premise, that these seven personal gifts named in Romans 12:6-8 are not something given or developed later in life: rather, every person is born with one. It is a Holy Spirit gift endowed at conception, and the characteristics of each of the personal gifts can be evidenced early in a child's life. This was true of my youngest son, David. Very early in his life he began to evidence the characteristics of one possessing the personal gift of prophecy.

From infancy David not only seemed to be absolutely fearless; but he was also able to withstand, and at times ignore, pain. I remember how amazed his older brothers and sisters and I were at David's stoic fortitude when he contracted spinal meningitis at the age of four.

As David grew older, I was often concerned about his proclivity to storytelling, in which he usually embellished and exaggerated in order to be convincing. I scarcely remember when he first began "selling," but I vividly picture his sales exploits in the second grade. That year he produced and sold "flavored" toothpicks, touting the benefits to be derived from them so effectively, that most of the children in the school bought them.

In my book, *The Idea Book for Mothers* (Tyndale House, 1981), I related this incident from David's life which was typical of his aggressive leadership. As trustee of our school board, I was once asked to spend part of a day on the congested playground to observe some problems. During one recess, I observed a number of boys crowding around a petite girl, waving their arms and shouting angrily.

I noticed that the louder they shouted and gestured, the more defiantly Teresa tossed her long, blonde hair. Moving closer to the fray, I soon perceived the problem. The boys were playing a war game in which Teresa desired to participate. But the boys were refusing her the privilege because, "You're a girl!"

The situation had reached an impasse, when a slender fifth-grade boy appeared on the scene. It was my son, David Lee. He instantly assessed the situation and took command.

"Quiet down, you guys," he said in a low voice that quickly penetrated the tumultuous wrangling. "You're just wasting time."

He motioned with his hand. "You guys be the Defenders. The rest of us will take you on. You've got two minutes to get ready. Now, get going!"

He turned to the remaining group. "OK, we'll take them! Teresa, you're my first lieutenant. Let's get going!"

Within a minute, order had been restored. Though there was some muttering in the ranks, everybody obeyed David's commands. As the leader's mother, I was spellbound by what I had just seen.

I heard a teacher speaking in my ear. "You've just witnessed one of our most difficult problems in action," she said. "What David does or says is *law*. Unquestioned law. Some of the kids love him. Many hate him. But they all obey him. I don't understand . . . I just don't understand. . . ."

She walked away, shaking her head.

I hadn't understood this phenomenon at first either. But I knew that from my son's very first social interactions, it had been obvious that there was something about David, a certain intangible something that made him different from my other children. There was a quality about him that attracted or repelled. He was strong-willed, determined, assertive. Other children and adults were seldom neutral about David. As the playground teacher said, they either loved him and followed him, or they hated and tried to reject him. But they could not ignore him. Wherever he was, whatever he did, he was very much a part of the action.

He seemed to thrive on confrontation and debate. The subject matter was immaterial, as was his knowledge or lack of it. He would debate anything and everything: from the number of geese in the V-formation, to the color of egg yolks (are they yellow-orange or orange-yellow?).

Admittedly, I often despaired of ever knowing how to handle this child who was so aggressively different from his brothers and sisters. He seemed so confidently inflexible, such an absolutist (often in total ignorance of the matter at hand), totally unwilling to compromise.

I learned to be very, very careful in my choice of words when I spoke to him, because he had the sometimes disturbing ability to recall my exact words to him in any situation. Later he would quote them to me verbatim if I attempted to alter my stance or statement. Despite all this, there was such an ineffable charm about the child that it was difficult to resist him.

During his early teen years, David turned his back on the Word of God and refused to walk in obedience to it. Nevertheless, his personal gift of prophecy was apparent in his total approach to life, though for a time it was perverted.

For a few years his provocative and radical nature touted ungodly living, and as a result of his boldness, confidence, and authority, he led a number of young people down wrong paths.

But at age nineteen, David made a turnaround. With no overt pressure from myself or my husband, he announced one day that he had made "an irrevocable decision to obey everything I read in God's Word."

And he has done exactly that—with no fear or compromise, believing that black is black and white is white (there is no gray), and what God's Word says is exactly what it means.

Today, as I am writing this chapter, David is joyfully teaching an open-air Bible study on the campus of Santa Monica College, despite any jeers or pressure from his peers. It was his idea, given to him from the Holy Spirit, which he boldly obeyed.

Because his personal gift of prophecy does not allow him to yield to the negative opinions of others, David has the unusual capacity to stand alone. It matters not what others think or say. When God has shown him from his Word that "this is the way, walk ye in it," that's exactly what David does.

He speaks the Word boldly to *everyone* he talks to, whether it be a peer, a professor, a man on the street or in the gutter, or the salesperson who is selling him shoes or gasoline.

David, as an example of one with the personal gift of prophecy, has no compunction about confronting strangers with their sinful life and urging them to repent—without any introduction or "warmup."

Though this "absolutist" style of operating has its advantages, it can also be a hindrance to the faith and growth of others. This has often been illustrated in Art Blake's home.

On one occasion, Art's daughter, Phyllis, and members of her Sunday school class had made plans to go to the beach for a day of witnessing. The skies were overcast when they left Pasadena, but by the time they reached Santa Monica beach, the weather had turned cold and windy.

"I have a suggestion," Phyllis said. "There's a shopping mall just up from the beach. Let's go there and pass out tracts." The idea appealed to the group, so they did so.

When Phyllis returned home her father asked, "What happened as you witnessed on the beach?"

"The weather was too cold," she said, "so we changed our plans and went to the mall and passed out tracts."

Her father was upset. "You went to the mall and passed out tracts? Just because of the weather? Do you mean you compromised your plans to go to the beach to talk about the Lord . . . ?"

"But, Father . . ." Phyllis began.

He wouldn't listen. "The Word of God says to be firm, immovable in the work of the Lord, not swayed by personal whims."

With tear-filled eyes, the girl looked at her father in amazement. Art Blake's personal gift is prophecy. But in this case, he was so absolutist in his style of parenting that he viewed any change of plans his children made as negative compromise.

As with the above illustration, there are numerous aspects concerning the personal gift of prophecy (which is also true of the other six personal gifts) in which misunderstandings can occur. So I'll advise you of this possibility by raising a couple of "red flags" for parents to be aware of. One of these has to do with the unusual capacity for the courage and ability to stand alone (a characteristic of those with the gift of prophecy), which can become an attitude of self-sufficiency.

Virginia was a sophomore in a new high school. So when she asked permission to go to a private party in the home of a girl whom her mother did not know, the answer was a firm, immediate "No."

"But, Mother, I want to get acquainted," Virginia wailed. "You don't know what it's like not to know anyone. . . ."

Virginia's mother paused in her dinner preparations. "I don't see what difference that makes. You should be able to stand on your own feet, and be your own person. . . ."

"But *I am* my own person. Even so, I need friends. Everybody needs friends. Otherwise they'll think you're . . . you're, well . . . stuckup," she ended tearfully.

"I don't need others to like me," the mother said. "I know what's right, and that's the way I live. If others don't understand or like me, that's their problem, not mine."

Virginia's mother has the personal gift of prophecy. And because she doesn't understand her daughter's personal gift, she has taken a "hard line" stance, based on her own personal gift. In this particular situation, the mother's lack of understanding made no allowance for her daughter's social needs.

Another "flag" for parents to be aware of is the danger of becoming inflexible because of their own strong personal opinions. Henry's father was one who fit this category. Henry had decided high school was not for him, so he dropped out in his junior year.

Henry's father laid down the law. He said, "You'll either go back to school or else you and I will go down to the recruiting station and sign you up for the armed forces."

"But, Dad, my grades are failing. You know that. It's terribly discouraging and embarrassing to sit in class and not know what's going on . . . especially with kids snickering all around you."

"Then study harder. I believe that anybody can make it in school if he wants to."

"Dad, you know that school's always been difficult for me. I never learned to be a student like you; so I've been thinking I'd like to take some vocational training and become an auto mechanic."

"My son, an auto mechanic! The answer is no, absolutely not! Either be back in your high school class tomorrow or we take that trip to see the recruiting officer."

What Henry's father failed to realize was that Henry had been demonstrating for several years that he wasn't making it in high school. And now in the crisis situation, the father's inflexibility was forcing him into a no-win situation.

Throughout this chapter, I've given examples of people—professionals, children, and parents—who possess the personal gift of prophecy. Frequently those possessing the personal gift of prophecy choose to follow such professions as: military leaders, crusaders, strategists, editorialists, teachers, pioneering researchers, political leaders, engineers, or even satirists. However, a person with any of the other personal gifts could also choose these professions. So, unless one meditates carefully, he could easily confuse a *learned skill* with a *personal gift*.

The two are not the same, though they have often been used interchangeably.

I noted an example of how this can happen while I was working on a special project with the Michigan State Board of Education. A man I will call Joe had been elected to represent the Upper Peninsula area of Michigan. Joe, an articulate college professor, persuasively campaigned for new and additional programs in his area. In fact, he *more than campaigned,* he crusaded! And he did so with such seeming confidence that he was eminently successful in his political undertakings.

If one were simply to observe Joe in action and listen to his strongly expressed opinions, he might conclude that his was the gift of prophecy. However, as I began to know Joe better, a different Joe began to emerge. And I saw, instead of the powerful, highly developed debater, a loving, caring man, who was deeply touched by the hurts of those around him.

As we discussed this seeming "Jekyll and Hyde" personality, Joe confided in me that he had decided early in life that the best way he could help his family and friends, was to become well educated. Then he could institute changes by communicating his ideas in the political arena.

"I studied the man who previously held the office I now hold," Joe told me. "And I began developing in my own life the personal characteristics that I saw working effectively in his."

"You seem so different, now that I've gotten to know you," I told him.

"The man you see before you today is the real Joe," he said. "Every time I stand up to speak, I am fearful and I cry on the inside. And every time I stand alone on an issue, I wish I were back in the safety and security of my own home. There is no joy in the doing of my job. Only the joy of *having done* something for my people—when the job is finished."

I realized then that Joe's high-profile approach was not naturally his, but rather one that he had spent much time and effort to develop. After discussion, Joe admitted that it was only when he operated in accordance with his personal gift of mercy that he had true joy. It was evident that his professional political position caused Joe a great deal of dissonance which he did not understand. This was because he didn't have a clear-cut comprehension of the individual personal gift that God had given to him, and to us all.

Joe's own *personal gift of mercy* motivated him to desire to help people and to relieve their suffering by caring for them. But his *developed skill* caused him to help people by taking strong political stands, accompanied by much confrontation, all of which would have been a joyful approach for a person with the personal gift of prophecy. But since these actions were so alien to Joe's approach of mercy, he actually suffered discomfort and dissonance.

On the following pages you will find the "Style Guide for the Personal Gift of Prophecy"—a list of eighteen statements delineating some of the most obvious characteristics and traits of a person possessing the personal gift of prophecy. The *content* of the list is not mine alone; it is the distillation of my work, along with that of other Bible students and theologians.

As you read these eighteen items, keep in mind that they refer to the manner, the style in which a person with the gift of prophecy *approaches any situation,* whether parenting or anything else. Once you begin to recognize your own characteristics, this approach or style will be very apparent in everything you do: in the way you deal with your children, your spouse, your friends, even with strangers.

It will be (and will become) apparent in the kinds of books you read for pleasure, in the type of people you enjoy the most. It will be the motivating factor in the jobs or positions you seek (whether salaried or unsalaried).

As you go over the Style Guide, keep in mind the fact that your learned skills might possibly fit many of the statements on the list. This is one of the reasons why a young child's personal gift is often more readily noted than an adult's—because he hasn't had time to learn or develop attributes that could possibly be confused with innate personal traits. The child would not have overlaid his personal gift with learned skills, nor have had time to submerge or pervert it.

In Chapter 9 I show how and why both children and adults sometimes pervert, sublimate, or submerge their gift. If you have done this, it will take time, meditation, and prayer before your personal gift will become clearly apparent to you. A word of caution is in order: Do not attempt to make an immediate decision as to whether or not prophecy is your personal gift.

Remember that these seven Style Guides (in this chapter and the following six chapters) can be used by anyone, whether Christian or not—because I believe every person is born with one of these seven personal gifts. However, since the gifts have been given by the Holy Spirit, I believe we need the Holy Spirit to help us recognize and fully appropriate them.

So read the list prayerfully, asking the Holy Spirit to impress upon you the traits, the style and approach he has given you. And as you do so, the Holy Spirit himself "will guide you into all truth."

Style Guide for the Personal Gift of Prophecy

1. Seems to have no fear.
2. Does not yield to what others think.
3. Has a strong will that draws/repels people.
4. Prefers and usually needs to express his message verbally.
5. Appears to exaggerate in order to convince.
6. Is an absolutist (all black or white).
7. His frankness may appear or be interpreted as harshness.
8. Is usually found where the action is.
9. At times appears provocative and radical.
10. Is quite persuasive.
11. Shows initiative and aggressiveness.
12. Does not like compromise.
13. Has unusual capacity for courage and ability to stand alone.
14. At times appears to thrive on confrontation.
15. Is sometimes viewed as inflexible because of his strong opinions.
16. Is a leader, sometimes a crusader.
17. Is able to withstand and at times ignore pain, stress, or persecution.
18. Displays great confidence and authority.

THE MINISTRY STYLE OF PARENTING

Have you had the experience of watching one of your children crawl across a linoleum floor without getting so much as a speck of dust on his hands or knees? Well, I have. It was at their grandma's house. Two words could be used to describe her floors—in fact, her whole house: dirtless and spotless.

But it wasn't just the scrubbed glow of everything in Opal's house that caught my attention the first time we met. It was the quiet joy that seemed to surround her; a joy that was apparently an integral part of everything she did—from washing dishes to serving fresh-baked cookies to helping me pick up the spilled contents of a bag.

There was something else. I guess you'd call it an expression of serious pleasure that was evident in everything she did—for me, and for everyone.

"Are you comfortable?" was one of the questions she most frequently asked. Indeed, it seemed that "making others comfortable" was a key motivation in her life.

Grandma Opal had the unique ability to detect and meet the practical and physical needs of her family and all who came into her home. She seemed to anticipate and care for all kinds of needs *even before they arose*. It was typical of Opal that she habitually sacrificed her own personal convenience and comfort to meet the needs of others.

However, in those early years of getting to know her, there arose a point of misunderstanding between us which had to do with the giving and receiving of gifts. As a matter of personal taste, I loved to receive dainty, extravagant, and even somewhat impractical gifts. Therefore this was the type of gift I usually gave. (This was before I had really internalized my own mother's gracious gift-giving philosophy: "Always give what the receiver would like to receive, and not what you would like that person to have.")

Opal, on the other hand, liked to receive (and to give) gifts that were practical or comfortably useful—such as a new paring knife or a soft pair of gloves.

If I had understood at that time that Opal's personal gift was ministry, then I would have realized that her total approach to life was geared to meeting the needs of others. I would also have recognized that Opal frequently used the socially established times of gift-giving (birthdays, anniversaries, Christmas, etc.) to meet some "practical" need of mine. And now, understanding Opal's personal gift of ministry, I can see that those very practical gifts that she presented me across the years were gifts in the truest sense of the word.

Opal is a homemaker who has always demonstrated a willingness to perform the most humble of tasks both in and out of her home. Her life has been filled with God-honoring service to others. My children's lives were blessed by having had such a grandma who positively modeled for them the personal gift of ministry. And in numerous ways through those years of raising children, my life was made much easier and more pleasant because of her.

During the months that it has taken to research and write this book, I have repeatedly been struck with the thought that the personal gift of ministry has not been fully appreciated in either the church or in society as a whole. This is undoubtedly due to an abysmal lack of understanding concerning the nature of this gift.

Which leads us to the question: *What is the personal gift of ministry?*

Within the context of Romans 12:6-8, where all seven of the personal gifts are mentioned, verse 7 reads, "[He whose gift is] practical service, let him give himself to serving" *(The Amplified Bible)*. The English word "practical" contains great depth of meaning; but because the word has become so "common" and overused, much of the word's fullness and richness has escaped our attention.

Some of the meanings supplied by the *Webster's New Twentieth Century Dictionary, Unabridged* are: "designed for use; utilitarian . . . concerned with the application of knowledge to useful ends . . . of, concerned with, or dealing efficiently with everyday activities." The following illustration will help clarify the above definition.

Frances ran excitedly into the kitchen where her mother was finishing dinner preparations. "Mom, guess what we learned in school today? Just guess!"

Charlotte said, "Something important, I'm sure. But I don't know, Frances. Tell me."

"We learned about the heart. And the blood. And arteries. All about the heart pumping blood through the body."

Charlotte smiled at her enthusiastic daughter. "Now let me ask you a question. . . ."

"OK, ask." Frances took a bite of a juicy apple.

"Did your teacher show you how to take someone's pulse so

you could determine how many times a minute someone's heart is pumping or beating?"

"No, Mom. But I'd like to learn. Will you teach me? Please?" She put her apple down.

"OK. I'll first show you how to take your own heartbeat. Take hold of your left wrist like this. . . ."

Within a few minutes Frances was able to take her own pulse *and* her mother's. "Now I'll be able to show something to the class tomorrow," she said. She gave her mother a hug. "I'm going to surprise Daddy by taking his heartbeat."

The Greek word translated "ministry" is *diakonia,* which means, in its most literal sense, service or ministering. It is used in connection with "those who succor need by . . . bestowing benefactions." Throughout the New Testament the word is variously translated "serving, ministry, relief, ministration, office, service."

Romans 12:7 in J. B. Phillips reads, "If it is *serving* others let us concentrate on our *service,*" which is the primary thrust of all the versions I examined. Without exception each translator rendered this word to convey the idea of "an act or action giving assistance or advantage to another." Thus, in context, the approach to a situation by a person with the personal gift of ministry is helpful, beneficial action or conduct. And the joy the person with this gift brings to any physical task involved in serving makes his presence a blessing.

It has sometimes incorrectly been assumed that the person with the personal gift of ministry is usually a homebody, and maybe even one who does not excel in any special field. This assumption is definitely not true. My friend, Mary Lou, clearly demonstrates the fallacy of that concept.

Mary Lou, who possesses the personal gift of ministry, is also a person with a multiplicity of artistic talents She paints. She enjoys interior decorating. She fashions exquisite party favors and table decorations. She is also an expert in creating and assembling decorator blinds.

Mary Lou is one of the most hospitable women I know. She cordially opens her home to others, especially strangers. Her hospitality is marked with a certain gracious quality that enables everyone to feel right at home almost immediately.

On occasion Mary Lou's home might appear disorderly, even unorganized. This impression, however, arises from the fact that Mary Lou usually has any number of projects in the works at any given time. This is partially due to the fact that she finds it difficult to say "no" to any request; which often leaves her so involved in meeting the needs of others that she might even neglect some of her own personal needs.

This remarkable woman has gained the reputation of being a tireless, indefatigable worker. Through the years, because of her driving desire to minister, Mary Lou has developed the unusual ability to remain cheerful while working hard and steadily under stress and pressure.

One of the benefits received by a child who has a parent with the personal gift of ministry is the cheerfulness with which the parent physically meets needs. This cheerfulness in meeting physical needs is also apparent in children with the personal gift of ministry who are meeting the physical needs of others.

Derek, at age seven, is an amazement to all who know him. He loves to "help" his mother in the kitchen and with the housework. He delights in raking the yard of the elderly man next door.

One of his friends, Evan, was complaining about having to dust the furniture for his mother.

Derek responded by saying, "I like to dust the furniture."

"You do?" Evan was aghast.

"Yes, really I do. I like to try and make the tables so shiny that I can see my face in them."

"Do you like to help your dad, too?"

"Yes, and my brother. I guess I just like to help people do things. . . ."

Though Derek doesn't know *why* he loves to help, his mother is already encouraging her son to feel comfortable doing physical things with excellence. With the personal gift of ministry and with the understanding of his parents, Derek's life and the lives of those he ministers to can only be enhanced as he freely gives of himself to others.

Because of their great joy in *doing,* those with the personal gift of ministry generally teach better by showing than by telling. Ann, who was once my neighbor, loved to teach her friends some of her skilled handcrafts. But she always did so with one of her finished works as well as an unfinished product in her hands. She actually did more showing than telling—typical of one with the personal gift of ministry.

Perhaps one example of teaching by showing with which most of us are familiar is the PE coach, who demonstrates more than explains whatever sport he is teaching.

Living next to a school playground for two years, I became acquainted with the school coach. I often witnessed him giving this type of lesson.

"OK, fellows," he'd say, "you've heard the man on the tape, do you get the idea . . . ?"

"You mean about shooting baskets, coach?" one of the boys asked.

"That's what I mean. Baskets. Shooting baskets. I'm going to demonstrate what you heard him say."

With the skill born of long practice, the coach dribbled the ball.

"Now I'm going to show you. Like this: with the tips of my fingers and thumb. Now watch. . . ."

The coach took aim and shot the ball—through the net. He lightly retrieved the ball, then dribbled it back. "Watch my hands, watch my hands." He aimed and shot again.

"Now, remember what the man on the tape said. Then *do* exactly what you *see* me do. All right, now, line up."

This coach (and any other teacher or parent possessing the personal gift of ministry) teaches best by demonstrating or showing instead of by verbalizing.

Another characteristic of the person with the personal gift of ministry is that he also most frequently expresses love by doing.

Joel went right to his room as soon as he came home from school. When he was called to dinner, he came to the table with a rather sober look on his face. His parents and Joel ate in silence.

Finally Joel's mother asked, "Did something upset you at school today, Joel?"

"Well, yes . . ." he said slowly.

Stephen paused in his eating and eyed his son speculatively, but said nothing. Julie persisted, "What was it, Joel?"

"It's science, Mums. I'm having trouble in science again." He laid down his fork. When he looked up, his eyes were filled with tears. "Mums, do you think I'll ever be good in science?"

"Of course you will, Joel. Of course you will."

Joel buried his head in his arms and sobbed. "I hope I can. . . ." His shoulders shook convulsively. "I sure hope so. . . ."

Julie got up from her chair and knelt beside her son. "I love you, Joel. Your father and I both love you. And you'll make it. We believe in you."

Stephen cleared his throat self-consciously and placed his napkin on the table. He quietly left the room. A few minutes later Joel and Julie heard pounding and sawing out in the back-yard.

When Joel got control of himself, he went out to see what was happening. His father was surrounded with sawhorses, boards, and tools. "What are you making, Dad?" Joel asked.

Stephen looked up and grinned. "A treehouse . . . where you can study your science . . . where you can *see* what you're reading about."

Those possessing the personal gift of ministry find great joy in serving others, as Stephen expressed by his actions. However, it is possible for one to desire to serve to such a degree that his actions inhibit or stultify the desires of others who want to be a part of the action.

Paul was pushing his bike up the driveway when his father arrived home from work. He pushed the bike into the garage and stood looking at it with a resigned look on his face.

"Having trouble, Son?" Paul's father asked.

"Yep. Got a flat tire."

"A flat tire? That's no problem. I'll change my clothes and fix it." Ten minutes later, Tom had the tire off and was looking for the hole.

"Let me help you, Dad," Paul said eagerly. "Let me help."

"This won't take long," Tom said, ignoring his son's words.

"What can I do, Dad?" Paul asked again.

"Nothing, really," his father said.

A short time later, Tom stood up and dusted his hands. "There, Paul, it's all . . . finished. . . . Paul, where are you?"

A brief search located the boy. He was in his room reading a book. "The tire's fixed," his father said.

"OK, thanks, Dad," Paul said, not looking up.

"Why didn't you stay there with me?" Tom asked. "It didn't take very long."

Paul laid down his book. "Dad, I *wanted* to help you. But you didn't need me, I guess, so I thought I'd just read my book. . . ."

There are other red flag areas of which the parent with the personal gift of ministry must be aware. A very common one involves the person who is so concerned about "helping others" that he may neglect his own needs. Or worse yet, he may neglect the needs of those closest to him, such as members of his own family.

Fourteen-year-old Clark was preparing to graduate from the eighth grade. He rushed into the house one spring afternoon with his hands full of papers.

"Mom, will you help me fill out these papers?" He thrust them into his mother's hands.

"What are they, Son?"

"My scheduling for high school. I need to plan my next four years so that I can prepare myself for that oceanography college I plan to attend."

"Well, put them on my dresser. We'll get to them . . . remember this is neighborhood spring cleaning month and I'm helping the Troys, the Browns, and the Moores." Marion looked at her watch. "I've got to get dinner started. Our guests will be here at seven. Clark, run to the store for me and get some. . . ."

"But, Mom, my schedule. . . ."

"We'll talk about that later; there's plenty of time. Four *years* of time. Quit dreaming about the future and help me with what needs to be done today!"

Some of the "doing" professions and occupations that seem to attract persons with the personal gift of ministry include: nurses, construction workers, printers, typists, waiters, painters, restaurant owners, and almost any service-oriented business or organization.

As was pointed out in the last chapter, some of the traits that characterize any of the personal gifts can be learned; which means it is possible for one to confuse his learned skill or profession with his personal gift.

My father was the oldest of eleven children. Very early in his teen life he found himself forced into the position of having to help raise his siblings, both by caring for them and earning money to support them. Which meant that early in his life *he learned to meet the needs of others* from absolute necessity. He had to work long, hard hours to keep the family together. And because the needs were so great and lasted for so many years, he found it impossible to complete his education.

As a result, my father learned to direct all available monies and resources toward the most pressing need. And all the needs seemed immediate and short range. There were no long-range plans.

It was my father's sacrifice that was instrumental in enabling many of his younger brothers and sisters to become educated and get a start in their own field of interest. Before all his younger siblings were out of the nest, my father had children of his own, which put even further limitations upon his time and aspirations.

My father became a skilled auto mechanic. He worked industriously and eventually was able to purchase his own service station. Each year he won awards for the cleanest and best-run station for the oil company whose products he merchandised.

But in all this "service" there was no true joy for my father, which is one reason why he looked forward to his retirement with such anticipation. I believe my father's personal gift is prophecy, *not ministry.* But because of his models and environment at the time, there was a perversion of his personal gift of prophecy.

As you study the Style Guide for the Personal Gift of Ministry, remember that anyone who is moving in accordance with his own personal gift will do so with great joy; while learned skills and professions may or may not bring joy. And in our society millions of people who do not have an understanding of the nature of their personal gift are likely to find themselves trapped in a basically joyless existence.

So don't make a hasty decision about your personal gift. Read the list carefully. Wait on the Lord, by binding yourself to his Word; then his Holy Spirit will direct you into all truth.

Style Guide for the Personal Gift of Ministry

1. Has the ability to detect and meet the practical and physical needs of others.
2. Willingly performs any task that needs doing.
3. Most easily learns by doing.
4. Will cheerfully inconvenience himself to meet the needs of others.

5. More readily expresses love by doing.
6. Is very flexible.
7. May be so quick to meet another's need that he interferes with the other's development.
8. Most enjoys practical people and organizations.
9. Is a good follower.
10. Enjoys working with physical projects.
11. Is usually a good worker.
12. May appear to have an independent spirit as a result of his insistence on serving, as opposed to being served.
13. Often allows people to take advantage of him.
14. His eagerness to serve may appear to make him seem ambitious.
15. Reacts to those who do not help in "practical" ways.
16. May be so caught up in personally meeting needs that he excludes other people from helping.
17. Tends to be practical in all areas of his life.
18. Prefers and shows more interest in short-term goals.

FOUR

THE TEACHING STYLE OF PARENTING

Before I was five years old, my Aunt Kakie moved in with us. I don't remember how long she lived with us, but my early childhood memories were dominated by her.

Life had not been easy for Aunt Kakie, and since a young girl she had been on her own. With no one to help her, she worked her own way through high school and college, an unusual thing for a girl to do at that time.

Aunt Kakie was a school teacher by profession; and she was a "born teacher" because of her personal gift of teaching. She was my second mother, my live-in teacher, dictionary, coach, the "opener-up-of-the-world" to my eager person. She became my mentor, and I became her protégée.

She never opened her mouth

without teaching something to somebody, anybody nearby. And since I was usually there, I became the focus, the object of her teaching skills.

Aunt Kakie edited and corrected every word that came out of my mouth. (Aunt K. is largely responsible for my ability to think, speak, and write in a grammatically correct manner.) Everything we came across was subject matter for a "lesson"—everything I saw, everything I heard, everything I touched.

My aunt taught me the wonder of words. She instilled in me a thirst for learning. She introduced me to the quest for knowledge. Nothing was too common or obscure for an object lesson: the empty shell on the beach, for instance. With her finger in the sand, or her inevitable paper and pencil, she would sketch for me a picture of the tiny creature that used to inhabit this temporary house. Then she told me stories about how this little invertebrate used to move into, outgrow, then locate another, larger dwelling place.

When the sky became black and streaked with flashes of lightning, she would explain to me the phenomenon of thunder and lightning, thus abating my fears. During those stormy days she would lead me to the Florida beach and show me the cresting waves.

"The water will wear away the rocks and the sand," she told me. After the storm had passed she showed me the shoreline, pointing out the erosion, the result of many storms across past years.

"Water and wind will even wear away stone," she told me. I never forgot the object lesson.

When I told her my friend had acquired a new puppy, she asked, "What kind is it?"

"I don't know," I answered. "I think it's just a puppy."

Her response was to take me to the library and show me a book filled with pictures of every conceivable kind of dog. And from that beginning, she introduced me to books about everything! Such experiences instilled in me my constantly renewed love of books and libraries.

THE TEACHING STYLE OF PARENTING

Aunt Kakie's classroom was anywhere she happened to be: in a car, at the dinner table, walking to church. She never missed an opportunity to pour into my eager ears and eyes the benefits of her stored-up knowledge.

For me to answer her, "I don't know," about any questions she posed was acceptable—the first time. Such an answer might *possibly* be accepted the second time. But to answer the same question with an "I don't know" the third time was beyond her comprehension. Her thirst for knowledge was unquenchable. And for Aunt Kakie, to share what she knew with others was as natural as breathing.

Nothing could stand in her way of gaining yet more, newer, more complete knowledge about anything. No sacrifice was too great or expense too high to deter her from seeking understanding.

For Aunt Kakie, teaching was living. It was life itself. Her greatest joy, her all-encompassing joy, was to impart knowledge: to a room full of children; to an adult Sunday school class; or to a small child, by sketching words and sea creatures in the sand.

I realize now just how blessed and enriched I have been because of Aunt Kakie and the many others like her who have crossed my pathway—all of them possessing the personal gift of teaching.

There was Mrs. McCracken. She was a Pioneer Girls' leader who taught me Bible verses when I was in the third grade. Bible verses were important to Mrs. McCracken, *accurate* Bible verses. She had me recite those verses aloud until I knew them perfectly. Not a single word, no matter how insignificant (to me) could be left out. When I forgot even a "the" or an "in" or "at," Mrs. McCracken would make me repeat the verse correctly over and over until I remembered to include the missing word.

She explained to me that prepositions were important (I didn't care). She talked about the beauty of the English language when words flowed together correctly (I didn't care about that).

Meanings, too, were important to Mrs. McCracken. "All we

like sheep have gone astray," I quoted.

"What does *astray* mean?" she asked. (I neither knew nor cared.) So Mrs. McCracken carefully and precisely defined the word for me.

Today I thank God for this caring, godly woman who possessed the personal gift of teaching. I also thank God for every verse of Scripture she painstakingly taught me, which seared itself into my mind. I can still quote those verses accurately. And today, *I do care.*

There was Mr. Workman. He thought, spoke, and taught in a systematic, logical, sequential manner. He was a mathematician. He discussed everything, including his own chosen field, in a "line-upon-line, precept-upon-precept" method, building each word upon the previous, foundational words. Everything he said came out in a precise, thought-through way, as though it had been carefully planned and programmed in advance. Mr. Workman had the remarkable ability of being able to assimilate, organize, and systematically retain any amount of new information, all of it subject to immediate recall and replay upon demand.

And, although I personally never learned to enjoy assimilating and retaining masses of related and unrelated information as he did, Mr. Workman did inculcate into me the appreciation of this characteristic, which is so much a part of those possessing the personal gift of teaching.

There was Dr. Shosvich. He was a psychologist who taught one of my psychology classes in college. He had a predilection for thoroughly understood and accurately used words. I learned this from the comments he penned on my first psych paper. "Overly dramatic!" he wrote, "Overly provocative! Thus I have no confidence in the validity of either your subject or its treatment!"

I deserved his comments. I had neither sufficiently studied nor prepared my material, and had then hastily written the paper, planning to give him a "snow job." I quickly learned how someone with the personal gift of teaching reacts to one who mishandles (or inadequately handles) words. And I realized that this professor was especially sensitive to the fact that I had tried to use words which I hadn't yet fully understood.

Then there was Pastor Ross—teacher par excellence! He had an incisive understanding of and appreciation for the correct usage of Scripture, and an intense dislike of its misuse. Many of those present at his seminars were prone to hand out verses of Scripture at random, saying as they did, "I believe the Lord wanted me to give this to you."

Ross abhored this practice, pointing out that such handling of the Scriptures often abused the Word of God by taking it out of context. "And when you take Scripture out of context," he said, "you are doing a double injustice: one, to the Word of God itself; and, two, to the one to whom you desire to minister."

Pastor Ross' strong adherence to this principle led him to disregard or even discredit the teachings of some exhorters whom he considered to be guilty of "sloppy exegesis." As I listened to Pastor Ross, I was alerted to the crucial importance of the correct usage of all words, *but especially the Word of God.*

"Be certain of your context!" he would often say. "Don't take Scripture out of context to prove a point of view. Never! And if there's a question about the meaning or definition of a word, check the original sources. Let's always 'rightly divide the Word of God.'"

Good advice from one whose personal gift is teaching, especially to those of us who may possess a different personal gift.

Then there's my oldest son, Terry. As my first child, he often seemed to teach me as much (or more) than I taught him. After my experience with Terry, it was several years before I realized that all babies didn't respond immediately to everything they were taught, and that all preschool children didn't soak up learning like a sponge—and beg for more.

I even thought (having Terry as my model) that all children considered books their most treasured possession.

From the time he was two years old, Terry always carried a pencil and notebook around with him. His most frequent statement was, "Teach me. Now, teach me." So I taught him. And he learned. Then he again said, "Teach me. . . ."

Before he was three, he stood before the entire congregation of our church and recited perfectly three passages of Scripture, each with four to six verses.

Terry loved books of all kinds. He loved dictionaries, encyclopedias, atlases, books of records. And he was able to assimilate and retain masses of information from almost any book he read. He was a thorough reader and was impatient with anyone who did not read books accurately, or who skipped over seemingly extraneous details and illustrations.

His favorite games were quizzes and mental puzzles; and anything that tested his knowledge was a joyful challenge to him. He also delighted in attacking and solving all kinds of difficult games and puzzles. He would study and work them for however long it took to solve them, thus developing patience and self-control.

Terry responded very readily to external discipline, and at a very young age internalized that discipline, making it his own. He has since developed into a strongly self-disciplined young man.

What a delight Terry was! And how rewarding for a young mother to have such a son as her successful first. For years I thought he was the result of some special mothering expertise that I possessed. But now I know differently. And in retrospect, it is now very clear to me that a baby with the personal gift of teaching is himself an especially teachable child, because he thrives on learning.

The gift of teaching is one of the seven personal gifts God has generously given to his children. Let's examine it.

"Having then gifts [*charismata*] differing according to the grace that is given to us, whether prophecy, let us prophesy according to the proportion of faith; or ministry, let us wait on our ministering: *or he that teacheth, on teaching*" (Romans 12:6, 7).

"Let us wait on . . . teaching."

The Greek word for "teach" is *didasko,* which simply means "teach." The *Webster's New Twentieth Century Dictionary, Unabridged,* amplifies the word: "to train . . . to give lessons to (a student or pupil); to guide the study of; to instruct . . . to give lessons in (a subject) . . . to provide with knowledge, insight." Synonyms for teach are: impart, direct, instruct, inform, counsel, admonish, educate, inculcate, enlighten, advise, indoctrinate, train.

One with the personal gift of teaching, then, is one whose joyous approach or style is to teach, to share information or knowledge. The total motivation of the person with this gift is to tell or to show or in some manner instruct another.

A child whose parents (one or both) possess the personal gift of teaching is indeed fortunate. This will generally mean that their home will be richly supplied with books. In addition, tape recorders, writing materials, dictionary, atlas, encyclopedia, maps, and other kinds of communication devices and paraphernalia may also be clearly in evidence.

In such a home, mealtimes, working-in-the-yard times, or just about any "together" times will be used for instructional interaction. At these times, anything from the story of Abraham, the last space shot, panning for gold, or the life of Columbus may be discussed.

My friend, John, possessed the personal gift of teaching. His children thought he was a walking encyclopedia. John's daughter, Tammy, told her friends, "He knows everything about everything. . . ."

"That's right," her brother agreed. "Just this morning he told me how a helicopter flies. He even showed me how to make a model helicopter out of popsicle sticks, thread spools, paper clips, and rubber bands. And tonight he's going to tell us about the duckbilled platypus of Australia."

I realize that knowledge can be acquired by anyone who devotes himself to learning. Personally, I call my husband, Bob, my "walking dictionary and encyclopedia," because he has more knowledge on the tip of his tongue than any other person I know. However, Bob does not approach every situation in a teaching mode, as does John. And that's the marked difference between the two.

John's joy comes from instructing, informing, or educating another person, whether child or adult. On a personal level, John's gift is the imparting of objective instruction or teaching, in practically any situation.

Bob, on the other hand, would give a more subjective and empathetic expression of similar information; but only to those who have requested the information or who have indicated that they are willing to receive it.

Now, let's look at some parent-child situations that have to do with the personal gift of teaching.

Rick and his father were taking their usual Saturday afternoon walk in the park. This weekly event had become important to both of them. Rick's five-year-old curiosity was at its best and he was asking questions about everything, with his father happily taking advantage of the situation to share his accumulated knowledge.

Suddenly Rick dropped to his knees. "Look, Dad. Look at the ants."

The parent knelt on the grass beside his son. He didn't say anything at first, but simply observed his son's expressions of wonder as he watched the busy little creatures. Then he pointed to one of the ants that was half-pushing, half-carrying a burden that was larger than itself.

"Look, Rick. That one is carrying something. It's bigger than he is! What do you think it is?"

Rick looked intently. "It's a piece of bread, Dad! A *piece* of bread. What's he going to do with it?"

"He's taking it to the ant house."

"But, what for?"

"When he gets it inside the ant house, the bread will be stored and later eaten. He's taking the bread home for food."

The boy looked at his father in wonder. "Do ants eat the same kind of food that we eat?"

The man laughed. "They eat other things, too. But, yes, ants do eat many of the things we eat."

The father rose and dusted off his knees. "Come on, Rick, let's go see if we can find where they got the bread."

Jim wandered into his father's office late Friday evening and watched as his father opened first one encyclopedia, then another, making notes from the contents of each. Finally he spoke. "Hi, Dad. What're you doing?"

"I'm preparing to teach my Sunday school class."

"Do you need *all those* books for that?"

Sam laughed and rumpled his ten-year-old's hair. "Well, some people don't need all these books to teach a lesson. But I want to learn a lot myself."

"It looks hard," Jim remarked.

Sam patted the chair next to his desk, and Jim sat on it. "Jim, nothing's too hard when you understand how to do it."

The boy looked at all the books, the yellow-lined pad. "But it looks so . . . so. . . ."

"Complicated?" Sam finished.

"Yes, I guess that's the word. Anyway, it *looks* hard."

Sam smiled. "Jim, words are the most important thing in the world. Remember that. Words. Nothing can be accomplished without them. No buildings could be built. No fields could be plowed or crops planted. Everything depends upon words. . . ."

Jim's eyes grew large. "Words. They're *that* important?"

"That's right. And I love words. Big words. Little words. All kinds of words. Each of them has a story to tell. . . ."

Jim fingered one of the encyclopedias. "Daddy," he began almost hesitantly, "will you teach me all about words?"

Sam smiled again. "Yes, Jim. I'll be glad to teach you all about words."

Both of the above parents possessed the personal gift of teaching, which was evident in their style of parenting. They used every situation, no matter how seemingly unimportant, to share the joys of living, growing, expanding. How fortunate their children were to be exposed so early to the wealth of the universe—through those who possessed this special gift.

Nevertheless, just as I have raised some red flags in relation to the other personal gifts, there are also some potential areas of concern that parents with the gift of teaching should be alerted to. For example, it is possible for the parent's interactions with his child to be so overly filled with technical details that the child's initial interest could become smothered. After a few such learning sessions, the child might view his parent's monologue (if the parent is not careful, it will end up being this *instead of a dialogue*) as long-winded and boring. Such a possibility might even occur concerning some untouched food on the child's plate.

Rodney moved the piece of liver from one side of his plate to the other. "Eat it," his father said sternly. "It's good for you."

"It doesn't *look* good," Rodney said.

"But *it is good* for you," the boy's mother said. "It's very, very good for you."

"Are you sure it's good for me?"

The mother laid down her knife and fork and launched into a lengthy explanation on the nutritional value of liver. By the time she finished her lecture, fifteen minutes had elapsed. She picked up her eating utensils and took a bite of liver herself.

To appease his glaring father, Rodney tasted a small bite. He made a face. "It's cold."

In his intense desire to teach, it is possible for a parent's precise vocabulary or over-validation of facts to stifle the child's creativity. There is also the possibility that his attempt to be totally objective might appear to the child to lack warmth or empathy. In either case the interest is hindered.

An example of this might be for a child to ask his father, "What's a computer?" and for the father to launch into an explanation of microprocessor chips, disk drives, video interfaces, and software. The child, though initially interested, is soon over-whelmed and sorry he asked.

Early in this chapter, I mentioned that one of the joys of parenting a child whose personal gift is teaching is that child's "teachability." Such a child, I said, eagerly seeks knowledge of all kinds, soaking it up like a sponge. This means, of course, that that child will amass a great deal of knowledge through the years. There is the possibility in this case that the possession of such knowledge, if not properly handled, could result in prideful arrogance.

If this child develops the "always right" syndrome, making himself responsible to correct misinformation, misunderstand-ings, and imperfections in others' knowledge, it is possible that he might fall prey to a condition known as "hardening of the categories" and thus lose his teachableness. If that happened, the child would no longer be a pleasurable source of knowledge and information and might instead become an irritant to others by continually challenging their knowledge or depth of research.

Mothers and fathers with the personal gift of teaching are an invaluable asset to any child, and to society as a whole. These people's desire for learning and intellectual growth often impels them to seek such professions as teachers, researchers, math-ematicians, archaeologists, writers, systems analysts, scientists, and other related fields.

Here again, it is possible for one to develop a certain skill to such a degree that it could be mistakenly identified as a personal gift.

Bill is an example of the above statement. He is an educational consultant who is president of a public relations firm. His enthu-siasm for grappling with and solving problems caused most peo-ple to view him as being endowed with a tremendous gift of teaching. In the course of his work he would be invited to school systems that were experiencing difficulties. He would thorough-ly research the situation, determine the genesis and develop-ment of the problem, then write a report. In the report he would define the problem and give a step-by-step program for its solution.

Bill was diligent and dependable. His personality was viewed as being stable, primarily because of his self-control in volatile situations. All of these traits are usually resident in one with the personal gift of teaching.

However, the truth of the matter was that Bill intensely disliked research. He detested "explaining how the problems developed," and admitted that his brilliantly written diagnostic papers were always written by one of his staff members. He used to say to me, "Pat, I don't care how the problem developed.

"All I want to do is to plan the proper steps and speak the encouraging words that will put things back on track. Because I know from experience that when people and organizations get moving in the right direction everybody begins to feel better about themselves *and* their jobs. Then the whole thing will come together beautifully and right itself."

By looking at Bill's motivation, it becomes clear that his personal gift is not teaching. His great joy did not come from teaching, but from *encouraging,* a distinctive of one possessing the personal gift of exhorting (see chapter 5). How, then, did Bill seemingly become "wrongly slotted" regarding his gift?

Bill's father (whom Bill admired and desired to emulate) exhibited the personal gift of teaching. Therefore, Bill, in attempting to model his father, *developed the learned skills* exhibited by his father. Nevertheless, his great joy came from a totally different sector than his father's (as I have discussed above).

As you study the following Style Guide for the Personal Gift of Teaching, keep the above illustration in mind. Remember to examine your basic approach of operating in a situation, and *not* your learned skills. Keep in mind those innate traits of yours, the fulfilling of which bring you great inner joy. Read and study the list carefully and prayerfully, inviting the Holy Spirit to "teach you all things" and to bring into sharp focus the personal gift he has given you.

THE TEACHING STYLE OF PARENTING

Style Guide for the Personal Gift of Teaching

1. Likes to research in order to discover full meanings and explanations for his own personal benefit.
2. Enjoys checking out new information.
3. Often clarifies by giving opposing points of view.
4. Loves words and definitions.
5. Enjoys and is usually skillful in word games or studies.
6. Prefers teaching as the method for all problem solving.
7. Tends to present himself logically.
8. Is diligent and thorough.
9. Has the ability to assimilate, organize, and retain a very large number of facts.
10. Tends to test the knowledge of those around him, and may thus appear prideful.
11. Is usually objective, so may appear to be insensitive.
12. Tends to give detailed instructions to others.
13. May appear to others as one who thinks he is always right.
14. May appear to be overly critical because of his desire to correct misinformation.
15. Develops self-control and self-discipline at a young age.
16. Is seen by others as having a stable personality.
17. Likes to understand in detail.
18. Speaks with detailed accuracy.

FIVE

THE EXHORTING STYLE OF PARENTING

It had been a good day, I mused. In fact, an excellent day. I had finished the dishes, the children were in bed or otherwise occupied, and my husband was in his study-office, involved in pleasurable research. I was seated before the fireplace, my feet on a hassock, watching the effervescent, dancing flames.

My whole being felt enswathed in goodness. I thanked God for his presence, for the evident witness of his love. All was well.

Suddenly I remembered: last night had not been like this. Last night I had been weary, out of sorts, wondering how I could possibly go through another day. How could I *feel* so different this evening from the way I had just twenty-four hours before?

Leaning back, I recounted the day's happenings. . . .

It all began, I realized, with that brief radio message I had listened to after the busyness of breakfast was over and the family had gone its separate ways.

". . . after all, where does your strength come from?" the radio pastor was asking.

Then for a moment it seemed that he was talking directly to me. ". . . forget the dishes. Forget the housework. Forget all of the usual things . . . and just for a moment sit down. That's right, sit down."

I realized God was speaking to me through him. I obediently moved away from the sink and sat down.

"That's better," the radio voice said, as though he could see that I had obeyed his command. "Now close your eyes and imagine. . . ." I was to imagine I was on a grassy knoll overlooking a huge lake. In fact, the Sea of Galilee. Which I did.

I was to imagine that I was sitting with a company of many people—men and women and children—and Jesus himself was speaking to us. In my mind's eye I saw Jesus standing before us, his arms outstretched.

"And now listen to Jesus' words . . . words that are directed especially at you," the radio said.

I listened and I heard. "Come to me," Jesus was saying, "all of you who are burdened down with life . . . you're wondering where or how your needs are going to be met . . . all of you, come to me. . . ." He was speaking comfortingly to us.

". . . and I will give you rest . . . and I will supply all of your needs."

Five minutes later I arose from my chair, cheered by these words of encouragement. I heard myself singing as I finished my housework, made my grocery list, and prepared to meet Pam for lunch.

Pam and I had been close friends for years. I had given her the first draft of a manuscript and asked her to critique it for me. Relaxing before the fire now, I relived that meeting with a warmth that did not come from the hearth.

Pam had breezed into the restaurant right on time, my manu-

THE EXHORTING STYLE OF PARENTING

script beneath her arm. "Pat . . ." she said, patting the envelope, "this is the best you've done yet. I've marked the pages that I thought we should talk about."

When I headed home an hour later, my step was light.

I had just begun dinner preparations when the doorbell rang. It was Annie, my ten-year-old "helper" from next door. The girl's name should have been "Pollyanna" for obvious reasons, I had often told my husband.

She handed me a rose. "I just picked it," she said.

It was lovely. I put it in a vase. Annie sniffed. "You must be baking bread. It smells so good."

She followed me around for half an hour, spreading nothing but cheer. "Your table looks so beautiful. Mmmm! May I just taste your warm bread? It's always so good!"

A few minutes later, she smiled radiantly. "Thanks for being so nice to me. I'll see you tomorrow." And she was gone, leaving an aura of light and joy behind her.

Before the fire, I stretched and yawned, just as the clock chimed ten o'clock. I was suffused with a warm glow of peace and serenity—*so different from just twenty-four hours before.*

What brought about the difference? I asked myself.

It was people.

Three special people. All of whom possessed *the personal gift of exhorting.*

Because of them my day had been fulfilling. My children had benefited. My husband, too. And I had an awareness as never before that the unique qualities evidenced by the people who had touched my life today were uplifting, heartening, edifying.

The *personal gift of exhorting.* What is it? What does it have to do with daily living? But most of all, *what does it have to do with parenting?*

And what style or approach to parenting does one have who exhibits the personal gift of exhorting?

Before we can adequately answer the above questions, we'll first take a look at several renderings of the Greek word, *parakleesis,* that is usually translated "exhort" in the New Testament.

The King James Version speaks of one with this gift as "he that *exhorteth*" (Romans 12:8). The same person is called "the *admonisher*" in the Berkeley Version. Williams, in his "Language of the People" version, speaks of the thus gifted person as "one who *encourages* others," as does Beck, in his translation called "In the Language of Today." J. B. Phillips, in his New Testament in modern English, speaks of this gift as one used in the *"stimulating"* of the faith of others. And the New English Bible describes the one with the personal gift of exhorting as one able to *"stir* his hearers."

This same word, *parakleesis,* is used elsewhere in the New Testament as: consolation, comfort, and entreaty. So we can say quite accurately that the one with the personal gift of exhorting, from the scriptural definition, is one who admonishes, encourages, advises, and stirs up or stimulates the faith of others.

In other words, parents possessing the personal gift of exhorting will encourage or stir up the faith and self-worth of their children. These characteristics were modeled for me in the person of a young mother who strongly influenced me when I was a child.

I was only nine years old when I first met Jean Carlson. Jean had just moved to our town and started a Pioneer Girls' Club. Since I was old enough, Jean invited me to join the club, which I did.

Jean had four small children at the time, and I still remember that her house seemed to be in a constant state of disorder. Nevertheless, I loved to go to Jean's house, and could hardly wait from one week to the next for our Pioneer Girls' meeting.

Despite the chaotic appearance of her house, there was a warmth about Jean such as I had never known. She drew me to herself with that warmth. She was deeply interested in each girl (and older person as well) who entered her house. For the first time in my life I realized I'd found a person with whom I could share my dreams and failures. I knew she would listen, interestedly and noncritically, and her words to me, when she spoke, would be filled with encouragement and godly wisdom.

I always felt stronger when I left Jean's house, somehow fortified against the sometimes difficult world of growing up.

Jean possessed an instinctive ability to visualize a person's potential, and seemed to know exactly how to direct others in their walk with the Lord. She often prescribed the steps of action her counselees needed to take in order to achieve spiritual growth. To do this, Jean spent hours searching the Scriptures, to locate just the right words from God for each person: certain specific applications of the truth that would exactly fit the individual with whom she was dealing at the moment.

As a very young girl I remember being fascinated by the skill she exhibited as she sought and found in God's Word those precise principles of living that she so aptly applied to her life, to her own children, and to each of her Pioneer Girls.

At that early age I didn't know that each person had been given a personal gift that affected his approach to everything. But if I had known (as I now do), I would have realized that Jean Carlson most certainly possessed the personal gift of exhorting.

On a practical basis, the essence of her gift meant that if one of her children (or a neighbor's child, or even a neighbor) required a sympathetic ear or a word of counsel, then the dishes would wait. The unmade beds would wait. The vacuuming would wait. She would quite literally drop everything and become immediately, totally available when someone's counseling need came to her attention.

And while Jean counseled, the joy, the love, the warmth that exuded from that woman would permeate the whole house. When I would leave after such a time, I would remember that I hadn't really noticed (or cared) how her house looked. The glow that remained was the glow of the Holy Spirit, transmitted to me through Jean Carlson.

Jean knew her personal gift that the Holy Spirit had given her. She functioned where God had placed her. The result: in addition to all the spiritual children she nurtured (myself among them), Jean raised six children, who are all grown, with homes and children of their own. All of them are godly men and women.

The *charisma* or personal gift of exhorting brought joy to Jean, which was spread to all those who knew her. (This is true of all seven of the personal gifts listed in Romans 12:6-8.) Of course, it does not necessarily follow that one with the personal gift of exhorting will have a cluttered home. But it does mean that such a person's home will be open and he will be available to listen and give words of encouragement. A few more illustrations of this gift are in order.

The high school teacher was speaking to the obviously nervous student he had asked to remain after class. "I'd like to talk to you about your last paper."

The student tensed. "Yes, sir."

"It's the best you've done so far."

"The best? Really?"

"Yes, it is. Where did you do your research?"

The student relaxed. "My father took me to the Museum of Science and Industry. I spent the day there."

"If I were giving awards for the most improved student, you'd get the prize."

The boy grinned. "That's great. Thanks!"

"There's no doubt about it. You've got potential in this field. I strongly urge you to continue."

When the student left the classroom he was walking on air. His teacher possessed the personal gift of exhorting.

The boy stepped into the garage, where his father was tinkering with the engine of the family automobile. He appeared shy and ill at ease. After a few moments, the father sensed his son's presence and looked up.

"Oh, hi, Tom. Ready for school?" He straightened and laid down his tool. "Tom, you look great in that outfit. Really great!"

"I do?" Tom responded with an embarrassed laugh. "I do?"

"You really do. Stand back and let me get a better look."

Tom stepped back, pleased at the complimentary attention.

"Now turn around." Tom complied. "Tom, it's perfect for you.

The colors, the fit, the style. And you wear it like the good-looking young man you are becoming."

Tom was whistling as he caught the bus for school. Tom's father had the personal gift of exhorting.

"Mother, may I go across the street and play?" The girl's brown eyes looked questioningly at her mother.

"Not today, dear. You've been over at your friend's house the last several days. Why don't you stay at home and play?"

"Because Susan *needs* me."

"Needs you?" the mother paused. "Needs you? What for?"

"Well, she needs me to talk to her. She likes for me to tell her things. . . ."

This girl has the personal gift of exhorting.

"I'm sorry I got angry last night," Barry said. "I just got so frustrated because I couldn't understand the assignment. And I . . . well, I just took it out on you."

"That's all right. Do you understand the assignment now?"

Barry shook his head. "No. You've gone over it several times with me already. And I still don't get it."

"Well, I've got the time. Let's try it again."

Barry shook his head again. "No, it's not fair to you, Steve. You've got other work to do. And it seems that I'm always bothering you. Let's forget about it this time."

"Let's *not* forget about it. C'mon, I've got the time. Let's look at it again. I think you're about to see the light."

The two of them sat down and opened their books. Steve has the personal gift of exhorting.

Throughout this chapter, I've introduced people—professionals, children, *and parents* who possess the personal gift of exhorting. And in each case, this gift is manifested by the instinctive ability to encourage, to lift, to stimulate feelings of self-worth.

A characteristic that is probably self-evident in this gift is that it often expresses itself in *the gratis giving of one's time to explain, amplify, or clarify life situations for others.*

As you can see, all of the above traits expressed by persons possessing the personal gift of exhorting are very commendable.

However, to those possessing this gift, a note of caution is in order. There are some red flags that a person must be aware of—whether parent or otherwise—because the exhorting person could and sometimes does go too far and actually harms the one he is trying to help.

A couple of these "flags" will serve to illustrate the point. One of them is the fact that *often a person's willingness to become personally involved will take him beyond the point which time, knowledge, or even finances would justify.*

When a parent (or other so-gifted person) becomes overinvolved he can trap himself or herself into doing more to solve the problem than to help the individual. Let me illustrate.

A father I know who possesses the personal gift of exhorting was trying to help his son research and write a term paper. The son was not very highly motivated to do the paper. He said, "After all, I don't have to hand in a term paper. If I did hand one in I'd get extra credit. But. . . ."

So Dick's father offered to help. He counseled with his son, did research, and even began doing some of the writing. He became so entranced with the project that he failed to notice that his son was doing nothing at all, but was just "leaning back" and allowing his father to do it all. By the time the father became fully aware of his son's attitude, the paper was nearly complete, with Dick having contributed nothing toward its creation.

So the father shrugged his shoulders, finished it himself, and gave it to his son to hand in. Dick handed in the paper and received an "A" for his father's work.

The father's personal gift of exhorting had taught the son nothing; and it had cost the father a great deal of time and effort. So no one gained in the transaction, because the son, whom the father was trying to help, chose not to be helped.

Parents with the personal gift of exhorting should be aware of this possibility—with their own children, as well as with others they may attempt to help. Learn to recognize the symptoms, then back off when you see yourself becoming too involved with someone who does not want to learn to help himself.

Another "flag" for parents to be aware of is the danger of generating a greater dependence than is healthy—for either party—as shown in the following illustration.

Amy and her mother were very close. In fact, even though Amy was in junior high school, her mother still made all her personal decisions for her.

"Mother, tell me how to study for this test."

"Mother, I don't know how I'm ever going to get all my work done . . . will you help me?"

"Mother, you have such good ideas about how to solve problems. . . . I could never figure out a solution as well as you."

One day the mother awakened to the fact that her daughter was almost totally dependent upon her for everything. And she didn't know what to do about it. When she thought objectively about the situation, she realized that she was herself to blame, because she had allowed her personal gift of exhorting to motivate her to "overadvise" in the counseling of her daughter. She had "solved" so many of her daughter's problems that her daughter's ability to do these things for herself had become atrophied.

Parents whose personal gift is exhorting need to be very cautious not to elicit dependence from either their spouse or their children. Also, as Christians, parents need to be very careful not to usurp the place Jesus should have in the eyes of those whom they counsel.

Frequently people with the personal gift of exhorting will gravitate to such professions as psychology, psychiatry, counseling, or personnel directing. Let me remind again, however, that unless one is careful, he could easily confuse a learned profession or a learned skill with a personal gift. *The two are not the same,* though sometimes they are used interchangeably. I will give a personal illustration of this in the profession of psychology.

At the Veteran's Hospital, where I took a practicum college course, I met a practicing psychologist we all called Marv. Marv was beloved by all and was known to be a cheerful, patient, and joyful man. Almost everyone who knew him considered Marv to be an encourager, and he was told by many that he most certainly had been blessed with the gift of exhorting.

However, when Marv spent time seeking the exactitude of his personal gift, he learned that his personal gift was *mercy* and not exhorting. In retrospect, he discovered the source of his confusion. During his professional training he had had very close contact with a colleague whose personal gift was exhorting. Marv's high regard for his friend caused him to emulate much of his behavior, leading him to develop certain skills that are intrinsic to one with the gift of exhorting.

Time spent delineating the two gifts clarified the matter for Marv. At the core of the gift of exhorting is the desire to solve a problematical situation; while at the core of the gift of mercy is the desire to relieve suffering and disharmony—the purpose most evident in Marv's approach.

Another example is that of Lani, a school counselor in my niece Karen's high school. Lani was also considered to be a "Barnabas" (one who consoles or encourages) by most of the students' parents. However, Lani's personal gift was not exhorting, but *ruling,* or administration (which would have been understood by those who had a comprehensive grasp of personal gifts). Lani's approach to counseling was long-range goal-setting (a trait of those with the gift of ruling), and not immediate problem-solving (an intrinsic trait of those with the gift of exhorting).

As you go over the Style Guide for the Personal Gift of Exhorting that follows, keep in mind the realization that your "learned" skills will possibly fit many of the statements on the list. This, I reiterate, is one of the reasons why a young child's personal gift is often more readily noted—because he hasn't had time to learn or develop attributes that could possibly be confused with innate personal gifts. Keep in mind that we are talking about *the way one with this gift "approaches" any situation,* whether parenting or otherwise.

Let me again caution you not to attempt to make an immediate decision as to whether or not exhorting is your personal gift. Do with this list as you have done with others: read it prayerfully, asking the Holy Spirit to impress upon you the traits, the style, the approach he has given you. As you do these things, the Holy Spirit "will guide you into all truth."

Style Guide for the Personal Gift of Exhorting

1. Has the ability to choose words that encourage.
2. Enjoys utilizing life principles from stories.
3. Makes others feel good about themselves just by being around them.
4. Takes every opportunity to talk with others and thus may appear to be shirking his work.
5. Has the ability to encourage others regardless of his own personal circumstances.
6. Especially enjoys those who are eager to follow his suggestions.
7. Tends to need the company of others on a regular basis.
8. Enjoys one-on-one sharing and counseling opportunities.
9. Is motivated to personalize most reading material.
10. Consistently expresses enthusiasm.
11. Has a patient attitude toward involved problematical situations.
12. His behavior is usually consistent and dependable.
13. May waste time on those who want only temporary relief from their problems.
14. Shows a willingness to go the extra mile to help someone solve a problem.
15. May become more involved in solving another's problem than is the person himself.
16. May encourage a counselee's dependence upon himself to a degree that is unhealthy.
17. Shares personal insights in a helpful, meaningful way.
18. Prefers reading and teaching materials that are liberally sprinkled with practical examples.

SIX

THE GIVING STYLE OF PARENTING

Archie is one of the most generous people I know. A successful businessman, he gives of his resources freely. Scores of pastors, missionaries, and Christian workers thank him for his generosity. I have been in his home many times and am continually amazed by the ways he gives.

For instance, my husband and I were scheduled to be in Florida for a convention. We called Archie and told him we'd be coming. He said, "I'll meet you at the airport. How long can you stay with us? And, by the way," he went on, "*don't* rent a car. You can use mine."

Archie wouldn't take no for an answer. He and his wife met us at the airport, ushered us to their inviting guest room, immediately putting us at ease and at home. Then, when it was time for us to drive a hundred miles to our final destination, he handed my husband the keys to his new car. "Take it," he said, "it's full of gas."

Visiting friends and missionaries are always accorded the use of his cars, driving them a total of many thousands of miles each year. But he doesn't mind. "They're God's automobiles," he says, "and they're to be used by God's people."

His home is a regular way-station for "God's people," as he calls them. And dozens, sometimes scores of missionaries and pastors avail themselves of Archie's generosity.

Once when I was in financial straits because of an unwise judgment, Archie sent me a check *for $1,000!* With it came a note, on which he had penned, "If it's convenient to pay this back you can do so. If not, forget it."

It was about two years before I could return the money. But when I did so, there was no comment, and no surprise. Just, "Thanks."

Archie has the personal gift of giving. He gives money, lots of money, to the missionary organization that is closest to his heart. He gives to his church. He gives to individuals. He gives money freely, but he doesn't waste it. He dislikes waste of anything, of food, of time, of resources—or money.

Like so many others with the personal gift of giving, Archie gives, but it doesn't stop with money. He gives largely, unstintingly of himself and of all his possessions.

The New American Standard Bible renders Romans 12:8, "he who gives, with liberality." This rendering of the word is essentially the same in all the translations I checked. The word "give" comes from the Greek word *metadidomi,* which means "to share a thing with anyone, to impart."

Traditionally, this concept somehow has been transmuted in our thinking to mean large sums of money. Though it is true that those with the personal gift of giving usually do *eventually give large sums of money,* this is not always true in those early years (because it is evident that all children born with the gift of giving do not at the time possess large amounts of money to give).

However, the above description *is not* the primary criterion to be used in identifying the person with this personal gift—which becomes clear as we note these further definitions in *Webster's New Twentieth Century Dictionary, Unabridged.* Among them were, "to be the source, produce; supply; as, cows give milk." This latter definition excited me, because, even as cows *cannot help but give milk,* so the one with the personal gift of giving cannot help but give of whatever he possesses—whether it be food, automobile, clothes, information, or money.

The same dictionary also defined the word, "to make gifts; to be in the habit of giving." Most of us give on occasion, or even regularly; but the one with the personal gift of giving gives frequently. He is "in the habit of giving." This approach, this trait, this mode of his is habitual. And like the definition of the cow "giving" her milk, this person can't stop giving. It is a built-in part of his nature.

Some words that are listed as synonyms for "give" are "confer" or "grant." However, the words are not precisely the same. "Confer" injects the ideas of condescension, or of "allowing" something which *could be* withheld. To "grant" implies some sort of a ceremony, or the "giving" to an inferior person. It also presupposes a request of some kind.

But the word "give" which is our consideration in this context should be rendered free of such nuances and connotations. For the word "give" as used in Romans 12:8 is the essence—in fact, the quintessence—of the best possible construction of the word. It means to turn over the possession or control of something to someone, *without cost or exchange or barter.* It means: *freely;* i.e., with no strings attached.

My oldest daughter, Trish, has been blessed with the personal gift of giving. She was only twelve months old when her brother, Keith, was born. I was somewhat concerned about how she would react to a new baby who would usurp her "position" at such a young age.

But I needn't have been concerned, because, from the very first, the baby became an outlet for her giving. Trish showered her baby brother with everything she had, and seemed not to need either my encouragement or praise to continue on her selfless ways. And, interestingly enough, even as a young child, Trish was careful not to overgive. Whatever it was that she gave Keith, she would give him only as much as he would use.

If I gave Trish a cookie, she would peddle off on her tricycle and find someone with whom to share it. If she received a new coloring book, she would leaf through it carefully, page by page. Once I asked her what she was doing. She looked up, seemingly surprised that I should ask.

"I'm looking for a picture Grandmother would like," she told me. "Then I'll color it and give it to her."

"Are you looking for a picture *just* for Grandmother?"

She shook her head. "No. I'm looking for a picture for you. And one for my Sunday school teacher. And one for Granddaddy. And. . . ." She named a long list of people.

Then she colored the pictures one by one. When she was finished, she cheerfully gave them to the specific people she had chosen. Not realizing in those days what I now know about personal gifts, I was surprised at how much joy Trish received— not so much from *coloring* the pictures, but in the *giving away* of those pictures. Of course, I am now aware of her personal gift of giving which flows from her innermost being, and she does not withhold it any more than "a cow withholds her milk."

I always encouraged and assisted my children in making presents through their growing-up years. Trish was tireless in this pursuit. But I soon learned that it wasn't so much that Trish enjoyed the *making* of the gifts. Rather, she enjoyed the *giving* so much that she would do whatever it took in order to have something to give.

This trait of hers continually amazed me. One Sunday morning as I was playing the piano for the Primary Department of our Sunday school, I saw Trish watching a little boy who never had any money for the offering. She spotted his jacket, which was lying on the table behind him. As I watched, I saw her put something in the boy's jacket pocket.

THE GIVING STYLE OF PARENTING

When it came time to receive the offering, Trish raised her hand. "May I do it, please?"

The teacher nodded and Trish passed the basket from one child to another. Most of the children gave, but the one little boy apparently had nothing to give. He tried not to look at her standing in front of him, shaking the basket, making the coins jingle.

"Lloyd," she said, "Lloyd. . . ."

"Aw, I don't have anything," he said, embarrassed.

"Look and see," Trish said.

He pulled his pockets inside out. "See!" he said.

"How about your coat pocket?" Trish persisted.

Angrily the boy grabbed his coat and jammed his hand in a side pocket. I watched as his expression changed from anger to bewilderment. He slowly withdrew his hand and looked unbelievingly at the nickel and dime. While Trish stood before him patiently, Lloyd longingly eyed them both, then dropped the dime into the offering basket.

Trish smiled happily and walked on.

At a very early age Trish looked for ways to give without publicity or fanfare. And when she gave, there was only one condition: the item *must be used* by the recipient. If this condition was not met, she was inclined to pass by that person the next time when she sought other outlets for her giving.

The person with the personal gift of giving enjoys meeting needs without the pressure of appeals. He is alert to discover valid ministries and needs that might have been overlooked by others. He enjoys giving to unpublicized needs. He will often show a desire to support and encourage ministries that have demonstrated faithfulness in "little" matters.

He tends to emphasize the importance of outreach in church and fellowship activities. When our church started a clothing ministry, Kathleen went home and rifled everyone's closet, seeking useful items to be given.

She was selective. She didn't look for worn-out cast-offs, but clothing that could be received and worn with pride. Kathleen's father, whose personal gift is mercy, was also complimentary of the church for initiating such a "practical" means of helping. But it was Kathleen, with her personal gift of giving, who was impelled to become immediately involved in this new "giving" ministry.

All of us experience joy when we learn that a gift we have given is an answer to a specific need. But the person with the personal gift of giving probably experiences an even greater joy. And if this person is a spiritual believer, sensitive to the promptings and leadings of the Holy Spirit, then he will more and more frequently give as he is directed by the Holy Spirit.

It is also true that one with the personal gift of giving has such a built-in readiness to give, that he may be more than ordinarily sensitive to the Holy Spirit's directives to give.

Children with parents who are givers are fortunate—in several regards. They are blessed because they will be given to by their loving father and mother. They will be blessed because they will continually see God's giving *personified* in their parents. And they will be blessed because they see the blessings that come to the less fortunate when someone whom God has blessed materially, blesses others materially.

Thus they will see God's Word come alive as promised. "As it is written, He [the benevolent person] scatters abroad, he gives to the poor; his deeds of justice and goodness and kindness and benevolence will go on and endure forever!

"And [God] Who provides seed for the sower and bread for eating will also provide and multiply your [resources for] sowing, and increase the fruits of your righteousness [which manifests itself in active goodness, kindness and charity].

"Thus you will be enriched in all things and in every way, so that you can be generous" (2 Corinthians 9:9-11, *The Amplified Bible*).

Of course, the above Scripture passage is a promise to *all* of God's children who obey him. I have inserted it here, because this chapter deals specifically with those who give as an approach to everything they do, and who do so with joy. For when they give to God's work and to God's people, God himself promises to provide even more seed for even more sowing, which will result in the ability to give even more.

Mr. Bell exemplifies this scriptural principle. Bell was the owner of a successful machine shop, and as God prospered him more and more, Mr. Bell gave more and more. Sometimes, it seemed (to my husband, who knew the man) with reckless abandon.

As the Holy Spirit urged him to give even more, Mr. Bell asked God to show him, "how I can most effectively benefit your kingdom."

God impressed him to select ten or more Christian leaders each year and to pay their way for a visit to a variety of mission fields. One year, my husband Bob was among those who went. Mr. Bell explained to Bob why he did what he was doing. "God showed me that each of you men will go back to hundreds, or even thousands of people, and inject them with the 'world-parish' vision which this trip will give to you."

An interesting sidelight to this story is the fact that Mr. Bell's children all became involved in the missionary activities of a church and *learned* to also give of themselves and their means to further the gospel. All of them expressed gratitude for the "model of giving we saw in our father."

And all of them were blessed because they learned to be grateful—to their parents, and to God—for all the benefits they had had bestowed upon them.

Parents with the personal gift of giving tend to be very much aware of the need to express gratitude for the "givingness" of others. And they will often lead their children in doing so by writing and sending thank-you notes for favors extended or gifts given.

The parent with the personal gift of giving has an ability to be content either with very little or with very much. But he usually has very disciplined work habits.

A Chinese business friend of my husband's is a good example of this. Mr. Lee was born and raised in Hong Kong. His parents were very poor, and as a child Mr. Lee experienced extreme privation in every area of his existence. This became an advantage to him as he grew older, because he was able to sacrifice creature comforts for years while he strove for and reached his goal of becoming wealthy.

No situation was too difficult for him as he fought his way from a street existence to wealth. Hardships had been the "norm" for him, so he was able to live on practically nothing as he put everything back into the small electronics business he established.

"He was one of the most disciplined men I have ever known," Bob told me. "And, even as a millionaire several times over, he lived simply. His apartment in Los Angeles' Chinatown wasn't any more pretentious than the suburban home we live in."

Mr. Lee was very generous with his wealth, though he didn't waste it. But his reasons for "cutting corners" in providing for his own needs were "so I can give to others who are less fortunate." And he gave generously of both his time and his means with great joy.

"One of the most interesting characteristics this man had," Bob told me, "was that he viewed time as even more valuable than money. 'Because what you can do with money is limited,' he had said, 'but what you can do with your time is beyond comprehension.'"

Interestingly enough, Trish has the same "time-saving concept" as Mr. Lee. And one of the most scathing charges she can bring against a person is, "He wastes my time!"

Another characteristic of the "giver" is one I've already touched on. Though he is generous with both his money and his time, he guards against the wasting habits of others. Mr. Conley is such a man. Mr. Conley was retired from his half-century of work on his several-thousand-acre wheat farm in Idaho.

Mr. Conley had scrupulously and laboriously parlayed the few original acres his father had deeded him into the prosperous spread he was farming when he retired early, "So I will have more time and money to give to God's work."

When he left the ranch and moved into town, his sons continued to work the land. But Mr. Conley, even in retirement, refused to waste either his time or his money. When his church began a building campaign, Mr. Conley gave generously to the project. But he didn't give the project *all* the money that was needed. He loaned the church many more thousands on a low-interest note.

Why did he do that? "Because," he said, "I wanted to help motivate others to get involved. I wanted others to receive the benefits of giving both money and time to advance the kingdom."

He was a model of his own precepts. During the construction of the church, this man of seventy was frequently on the job, dressed in overalls and a leather jacket, even in the most severe weather, doing common labor, "Where I am needed."

Once his pastor, Rev. Neuschwanger, asked Mr. Conley, "Why are you working so hard?" Conley laughed. "I'm not working nearly as hard as I worked on the ranch. But I want to be here with the rest of the volunteer workers—just adding to the kingdom's treasury."

There are, of course, dangers or "red flags" that parents with the personal gift of giving must be aware of. One is the all-too-common one of getting caught up in the money-making game, then measuring success by material assets. This was the trap Glen found himself caught up in.

Glen saved up enough money to purchase a small dairy. And as his business continued to prosper, he gave more and more to his church and to God's work. Then his emphasis began shifting.

My husband talked to Glen one day. "Glen, you and I've been friends for quite a while. And you're a member of the Sunday school class that I teach."

"That's right," Glen said. "What're you getting at?"

"Well, lately you've been so involved on Sundays that you haven't been to church. . . ."

"I still pay my tithe!" Glen burst out. "And I come Sunday nights."

"Some of the time," Bob corrected him. "What's happening to you, Glen?"

"Well, I've just bought that new milk processor, so I've had to buy another fifty cows to make it pay. . ." Glen began.

Originally, Glen's motives had been right. "I'm building a bigger business to make more money, so I can give more to God," he said. But it wasn't long before Glen no longer owned his business. It owned him. He no longer controlled his burgeoning bank account. It controlled him. And then he began to talk more about what he had than what he could give. The focus had changed.

Children, too, can "miss the mark" in this area. And even a small child possessing the personal gift of giving might fail to see the value of small beginnings. When he sees his parents giving many dollars in the offering, he might think, "My pennies and dimes don't account for much. So I'll just withhold them until I can give more."

And if the parents of the child with the personal gift of giving don't encourage the child in his small means of giving, then the child's joy may be stunted and his approach to giving might scorn all but grandiose projects.

As is true with all the personal gifts, those with the gift of giving can be found in almost any profession. However, in this case, there will be a special leaning toward positions that offer the opportunity to influence people who handle large sums of money. Examples of this are: bankers, investors, entrepreneurs, business executives, accountants, foundation administrators, property managers, and so forth.

When studying the Style Guide for the Personal Gift of Giving, keep in mind the importance of clearly differentiating between learned skills and professions and your personal gift of giving. Remember: when one learns his personal gift and begins to use it, it always brings him great joy.

My friend, Theo, was an administrative assistant at World Vision who loved to give to every new project. For this purpose, she kept a box on her desk with the sign, "To Help a Need." Because of her generosity and her intense desire to give, most of her friends and associates believed Theo possessed the personal gift of giving. However, Theo's giving was primarily geared to help alleviate suffering. Her deepest joy, though, came *not from giving;* this was but one medium she used to heal and help those in distress, for her personal gift was mercy.

Style Guide for the Personal Gift of Giving

1. Uses his material goods efficiently for the benefit of others.
2. Enjoys giving to unpublicized needs.
3. Receives his pleasure from the giving, rather than from any publicity or recognition.
4. Is alert to discover places to give and resources to utilize that have been overlooked by others.
5. Tends to give of his best rather than something lesser.
6. Prefers his involvement in organizations to be primarily of a monetary nature.
7. May limit another's opportunity to give to him.
8. Wants his gifts to have lasting benefit, to meet long-term as well as short-term needs.
9. Does not like to be indebted in any area.
10. Has an ability to make personal sacrifices in order to give.
11. Often prefers a supportive, behind-the-scenes role.
12. Tends to be sensitive to right timing in his gifts.
13. May appear to others to have an overly temporal value system.
14. Experiences great joy when he learns that his giving is an answer to a specific need.
15. Has an ability to function well either with very little or with very much.
16. Enjoys meeting needs without the pressure of appeals.
17. May appear to be trying to control through his giving.
18. Appreciates gratefulness and is sensitive to gratefully acknowledge the gifts and deeds of others.

SEVEN

THE RULING (ADMINISTRATIVE) STYLE OF PARENTING

I remember the first time I saw him.

He came striding across the platform of the Billy Sunday Tabernacle in Winona Lake, Indiana. He was a big man, imposing to my teenage eyes. Along with about 100 others, I was standing on the platform waiting for choir practice to begin. But we couldn't start, because the choir director was late.

So this man stepped up to the microphone. "Time is a gift from God, and YFC'ers shouldn't waste it," he said. He dispatched a young man—on the run—to locate the choir director. He appointed a temporary choir director and pianist. Almost immediately order was restored and choir practice was in progress.

It was years before I saw him again. This time it was in California. I had been invited to give some lectures on goal-setting for the National Christian Secretaries' Association. Rex, the president of NCSA, and I had a business appointment with "the man," and we soon found ourselves being ushered into "his" office. He was everything I had remembered, only more so. He was totally organized: his personal appearance, his office, his secretarial staff, even his very logical, precisely spoken words.

The last time I saw him, just two weeks ago, was when Bob and I visited him and his wife in their vacation home. Again I was struck by the bigness of the man—big in every dimension. And I was intensely aware of his recognition and acknowledgment of the achievements of others, especially of those who had helped him in achieving his goals.

What more appropriate example could I use in this chapter to introduce the personal gift of administration, than Dr. Ted W. Engstrom, president of World Vision International.

Dr. Ted possesses the rare ability to integrate numerous ministries, people, tasks, and/or projects, shaping and welding them into a single unit for the purpose of fulfilling a long-range plan or goal. He has the ability to visualize the project's (or organization's) overall needs, and to crystalize and clarify them so they can be divided, delegated, and accomplished.

So it is that Dr. Ted—nearly thirty years after my first contact with him—is still reminding those around him "to redeem the time." This man models his motto. He manages his own time superbly, urging and teaching others to do the same: in person, through the books that he writes, and through his unique, well-attended "Time Management" Seminars.

Dr. Ted is motivated to delegate, if at all possible, and he instinctively knows what can or cannot be effectively delegated. He places the highest premium upon reliability and responsibility. He insists upon total, thorough planning and organization before embarking on any new task or ministry. He avoids "like the plague" the so-prevalent, "develop-as-you-go" thinking concerning anything. He insists that things be done correctly, with excellence, from the very outset.

Dr. Ted Engstrom exemplifies the Bible definition of the personal gift of ruling (or administration) given in Romans 12:8. "He who gives aid and superintends, [let him do it] with zeal and single-ness of mind" *(The Amplified Bible)*. The King James Version calls this sixth personal gift in the Romans 12 list, "ruling," and says of it, "He that ruleth, [let him do it] with diligence."

The "ruling style," or "style of ruling"! It sounds rather bossy, doesn't it? That's how those exhibiting this personal gift of ruling are often viewed by others: bossy. When I was a little girl, my friends used to sometimes call me "Bossy," and perhaps rightly so. When I had chores to do, I often figured out a way to motivate my friends to help me (or, better yet, to "do them" for me). When a teacher gave us a homework assignment, I would delegate various portions of it for my friends and myself to do, so that all of us got it all accomplished for maximum benefit, with minimum effort.

This personal gift is the one that designates a managing approach. It derives from the Greek word *proisteemi,* and is variously translated, "ruleth, takes the lead, to be over, to super-intend, preside over, administrative ability."

My own personal gift is administration. Consequently, I approach everything I do from that point of view. I assess the work or situation, consider all the people involved, then delegate.

As the mother of five children, all just a year or two apart in age, I had my hands full of children all the time. It was fortunate for me that I was an organizer. From the time my children could crawl, they each had their own "place" or drawer in the kitchen, which was theirs alone. They were totally responsible for its care and everything that went into it. And each child, by the time he had reached the age of three, was also responsible to perform his own regular chores around the house.

I was well organized. And I saw to it that my "crew" was well organized. I posted their schedules on the refrigerator. For the pre-readers, I drew pictures or made visuals depicting each child's area of responsibility. For example, one child had the week-long responsibility of setting the table. I clipped pictures describing this scene from a magazine and posted it beneath his name, which he was able to identify by this age. I did the same with washing dishes, making beds, mowing the yard, feeding the fish or dogs, etc.

In retrospect, I can see how blessed I was to have had the personal gift of administration, which enabled me to effectively regulate a house full of children. Although I was always very busy, I was never overwhelmed—because I delegated everything that could be delegated to each child as soon as he grew old enough to successfully accomplish the task.

Because of such discipline and delegation, each of my children early learned to organize his own affairs, which made it possible for our household to function in an efficient, unhurried, quiet, orderly manner.

One of the characteristics of the parent with the personal gift of administration is the ability to discern or determine the talents and resources of his own children, as well as others. By so doing, this parent will be able to assist his children by designing and setting up options that will provide the greatest personal satisfaction and enable them to make the fullest use of their talents and resources.

Since my personal gift is that of administration, there was a compelling within me to find outlets through which I could enable each of my children to be or to become individually successful. With Terry, my oldest, I spent many hours teaching him Scripture and poetry, and coached him in reading and memorization. Later, when he was a sophomore in high school, I even enrolled in the Glen Oaks Community College for a class of elocution.

With Trish, I studied acting, skits, and monologues in order to help utilize an outlet for her ready wit. Keith showed an aptitude for singing, which I fostered and encouraged by finding opportunities for him to perform and people to give professional assistance. Alice loved animals, especially poodle dogs. She was given a poodle and the two of them were enrolled in obedience training which qualified them for competition shows. With David, the youngest, there was a need to excel in some area different from his brothers and sisters. We enrolled him in a military academy which gave him opportunity for personal achievement through officer's training.

My greatest joy came (and continues to come) from my motivation to help my children and others to utilize their potential and become personally successful.

The parent with the personal gift of administration places a high premium on reliability and responsibility. This is true even though he will himself avoid the limelight, enjoying the role of "strategic commander" who works behind the scenes and calls the shots. And he is somewhat inclined to become irritated with those who do not follow through and help with the "cleanup" or other behind-the-scenes work.

The parent with this gift tends to remain firm and steadfast, regardless of opposition. Once he has determined that a particular goal or objective is "right," he becomes immovable. He believes strongly in keeping commitments, even in the face of adverse or seemingly impossible circumstances. He has the added trait of being able to finalize all decisions, even difficult ones.

For example, Jack had given his twelve-year-old twins until April 1 to make up their minds about summer camp. "If you haven't chosen between the beach or the mountains by that date, I'll make the decision for you," he had told them early in the year.

Now it was D-day and the two were still discussing the matter. "I think we'll get the most good from the mountains," Peter said. "Just think, we can ride horses, we can fish. And swim. We can even hike."

"We could do all of that at the beach," Paul countered. "Well, most of it. And you can surf at the ocean, which you can't do in the mountains. You've got to admit that."

"Well, we've got good friends in the mountains ..." Peter said.

"And at the beach. . . ."

Just at that moment the door opened and the boys' father walked in. "Made up your minds yet?" he asked.

"I want to go to the mountains," Peter said.

"And I think we should go to the beach," Paul said.

Their father looked from one to the other. "OK, you are indecisive, so I will make the decision. Peter will go to the mountains. Paul will go to the ocean. It's settled." He turned to go.

"But, Dad," Paul said, "we've never been apart before."

Peter said, "We don't want to split up, Dad."

Their father spoke firmly. "I didn't split you up. The two of you haven't been able to come to agreement in two months. Indecisiveness always allows external forces to make your decisions for you. It is settled." He closed the door firmly behind him.

The person with the personal gift of administration receives great fulfillment in seeing all the pieces of a project fitting together, and watching others enjoy the finished product. However, once the project is completed, he quickly loses interest, and is ready to move on to a new challenge.

The above statement can be illustrated by the following example. Martin was an expert fund-raiser who had just completed ten years as Vice President of Financial Affairs at a Texas college. He came home one day quite excited. "Christine, George just called me from Chicago."

Christine looked up from her sewing. "Oh . . . what about?"

"He offered me a job . . . consulting."

Christine put her hand to her throat. "You didn't consider it, did you? After all, we've gotten settled here. Our friends are here. . . ."

Martin paced the living room. "That's right, Christine. And I've licked every obstacle in my job. There's no challenge left. I've raised more money than the college can spend for the next fifteen years. I'm considering his offer."

"But you have a title . . . and. . . ."

"Christine, all that title means is that I'm in charge of administrating the new foundations."

"But what about all your retirement benefits?"

"Retirement? I'm only fifty . . . and I still need a challenge. Please, please try to understand."

When problems arise in a home between children, the parent with the personal gift of administration will be quick to restore order. He frequently does it by readjusting responsibilities between children, in order to achieve more compatible working relationships. Or by resetting priorities or goals for each.

I can illustrate this from a personal incident which has to do with undesirable behavior at the dinner table. When anything like this happened in my own home, I simply rearranged seating positions. My Aunt Pat handled such a situation differently.

She and her three children came to visit us, and during the meal, her children became disruptive. As soon as the behavior reached an unacceptable level, she said, "Both of you leave the table and come into the living room with me."

They both got up immediately and followed her. I could hear her speaking to them. "Now tell me what happened," she said to first one, then the other. When each child had given his personal perspective on the situation, she said, "All right, now that we've got that settled, this is what we're going to do. . . ." She then outlined steps to prevent a recurrence of the disruption.

My Aunt Pat had acted from her personal gift of exhorting, which I didn't realize at the time. What I did think, though, was that her way was time-wasting and unnecessary. Now, if I had had to deal with the situation, I thought, I would have quickly moved Carol across the table from her brother. That would be it.

Now I realize that neither her way nor mine is best, only different. Today, in retrospect, I realize that there must have been times when my children felt "misused" or "misunderstood" because of my direct approach. As the above example illustrates, I usually didn't discuss feelings, I moved ahead and "did the job," despite what they may have felt.

Someone with the personal gift of administration tends to avoid involvement in anything for which he has no organizational responsibility. If the leaders in charge do not release any responsibility to him, he tends to remain on the sidelines. If no structured leadership exists, he will "take over" and assume responsibility, for such a person is strongly motivated to organize anything for which he becomes responsible.

These same traits are evident in children with the personal gift of administration. And these children instinctively approach any situation as I have described above. For example, I remember watching a mother who had just enrolled her child in our school, urging him to "get involved" in a school playground activity. The child hung back and refused. But when the teacher offered a leadership position, the child responded immediately. Within minutes he was calling the shots and determining the game plan.

Of course, as with the other gifts, there are "red flags" to be aware of and to avoid. One that comes to mind can be illustrated with an example that has occurred in my house. Though Bob and I are both writers, and often work together on the same project, our writing methods are different.

Bob tends to pace himself and work at a steady, measured gait all the time. Whereas, I am so project- or task-oriented, that I tend to brush aside all schedules, personal feelings, and needs, and "push ahead" to complete the project. This tendency sometimes results in great weariness for us both. I am learning to be or become more considerate of Bob's working schedule and to not push us both too hard.

Because the one with the personal gift of administration tends to avoid small talk and lengthy explanations, his supervision of others on a project can result in resentment. Some space or "room" must be left for some interaction or explanation concerning tasks, or people may feel they are being "used" as mere resources or "tools" in a project, instead of being worthwhile people in and of themselves. And since the "ruling" person thus described is able to endure reactions and criticisms from others in order to accomplish a goal, he may sometimes appear calloused and insensitive.

My husband tells of such an incident that occurred while he was sailing as a deck officer in the Merchant Marines. Their ship was docked in Sydney, Australia. The captain had given my husband orders to see that the superstructure of the ship was painted by the crew during the ship's stay in Sydney. His only statement as he went ashore for the week was, "I want her to look good when we sail into San Francisco." When Bob faced the already battle-weary crew with this huge maintenance task, there was much resentment expressed. Because the captain showed no awareness of the men's needs, there was an additional drop in the morale of the crew.

Some of the professions that tend to attract a person with the personal gift of administration are: administrators, contractors, managers, efficiency experts, personnel directors, business executives, and superintendents.

As you study the Style Guide that follows as a means of determining if the gift of administration is yours, I again remind you that such a determination is not a simple question-and-answer routine. It is possible that you may possess learned skills or abilities that could conceal or mask your own personal gift. Keep in mind that when you determine your own personal gift, it is one that, when exercised, will bring great joy to you.

My oldest daughter, Trish, is an example of one who very early exhibited a learned skill. Because of her great admiration for me, she has patterned her own behavior after mine since she was a tiny girl. During her school years, she sought for and achieved such "leadership" administrative positions as cheerleader and yearbook editor, and excelled in both.

After graduating from college and a specialized travel school, Trish accepted the position of tour guide with an incentive travel agency. Among her other responsibilities, Trish would help orchestrate trips for as many as 50 to 1,000 people, by planning and expediting the trip arrangements. Because of her ability to handle such demanding assignments so efficiently, all those who knew her assumed that her personal gift was administration, as was her mother's.

However, such is not the case. As I related in chapter 6, Trish's personal gift *is not administration;* it is *giving.* Though she does excel in administration, her joy comes from giving. With the completion of administrating a job well, there is satisfaction for Trish. But in giving, *there is immense joy.*

Style Guide for the
Personal Gift of Ruling/Administration/Organization

1. Has an ability to visualize overall needs.
2. Possesses an ability to integrate several tasks, projects, and people into a common goal.
3. Has an ability to involve people in a way that best utilizes their talents.
4. Tends to avoid involvement in anything for which he has no organizational responsibility.
5. Tends to assume responsibility if no structured leadership exists.
6. Prefers planning, rather than a develop-as-you-go project.
7. Is strongly motivated to organize anything for which he is responsible.
8. Will delegate whenever it is possible.
9. Tends to be neat and orderly in all aspects of personal life.
10. Is able and willing to endure reaction from others in order to accomplish a goal in a minimum amount of time.
11. Enjoys helping others become more efficient in carrying out tasks.
12. Appreciates initiative.
13. Will look for a new challenge whenever a project comes to completion, which may appear to be instability.
14. Demonstrates an ability to finalize difficult decisions.
15. May appear to be a perfectionist.
16. May appear to use people because of a tendency to treat people impersonally or view them as resources.
17. May seem insensitive or calloused because of his strong goal-setting/completing drive.
18. Tends to remain firm and steadfast, regardless of opposition, once he is focused on a goal.

EIGHT

THE MERCY STYLE OF PARENTING

As I face the blank sheet of paper in my typewriter entitled, "The Personal Gift of Mercy," so many faces from my own family flash across the screen of my mind. There's my husband, Bob; and my mother. There is Keith, my middle son; Alice, my youngest daughter; and my nephew John, who is presently living with us. All of them so different in totality, and yet their innate approach to everything is merciful. For each of them possesses the personal gift of mercy.

My husband, Bob: He has such a special desire and capacity to remove hurts and bring healing to others. He readily identifies with those in distress, and seems to know how and when to administer personal, tender care to them. He goes to great lengths to prevent unnecessary suffering.

Bob has a tendency to respond

emotionally to a situation before examining all of the facts. This is diametrically opposite to the way I respond. In chapter 7, on the personal gift of ruling, my own manner or approach to situations was illustrated: which is usually from a factual, objective viewpoint.

Sometimes Bob responds emotionally to a situation prior to establishing the relevant facts. On the other hand, I am more likely to respond to the facts, without adequately considering the emotions. So you can see, our home (as is every Christian home) is a microcosm of the Body of Christ. We complement each other. We strengthen each other. We add to each other. All of which illustrates the mathematical maxim that "the combined strength of two is greater than the sum of both parts."

Presently our home is filled with our young people (Trish, Alice, David, and John), who are often accompanied by their peers. So Bob's "space" is frequently intruded upon. But for the most part, Bob yields his personal rights and time with a joyful spirit. And when it sometimes becomes necessary for him to administer discipline, it's as painful for Bob (and perhaps more so) as it is for the one being disciplined. Because of his strong desire to empathize with one who is hurting, Bob actually finds it difficult to correct a problematical situation. And if he didn't consistently abide in and by the Word of God, he would find it easier to sympathize with the person than to correct him.

A special strength Bob brings to our home is the immensely beneficial expression of "touching." He values physical contact in his personal relationships. He desires to "feel" another person's emotional response as well as see it. Therefore he may use the elixir of physical touch to express his care and concern, to soothe away hurts, or to show his desire and willingness to protect.

Though Bob often uses touching as an emotional response, I seldom do. He is very sensitive to the body language of others, and is thus careful of his own. Harsh or inappropriate words or actions which would scarcely affect me could wound his sensitive spirit. Why is this? I believe it's primarily because of the difference in our personal gifts.

Let's examine this personal gift that's defined as *mercy* in most translations. The parent (or any person) thus endowed earnestly desires to comfort those in distress. He desires harmony in the home, or in any other situation in which he is involved. He seems to be equipped with a specialized tuner that picks up messages of emotional distress, especially from children.

Since this parent is sensitive to pain, suffering, and hurt feelings in others, his ears are keenly attuned to what is happening in the household. If a child is happy, he rejoices with him. If a child is sad or upset for some reason, this parent shows empathy toward him.

The Greek word that has been translated *mercy* in Romans 12:8 is *eleeo* and means "to console, to have mercy on; to succor one afflicted or seeking aid." The word is also translated "compassion" in several New Testament references.

So you can easily see that compassionate, caring concern is a primary trait of one with the personal gift of mercy. He will approach every situation seeking to ease any pain or suffering, whether physical or emotional.

For example: Bob was recently asked to provide leadership for an organization that has been set up for the primary purpose of assisting international students and caring for homeless or deprived children. It would be a heavy load, without monetary remuneration for time spent, but Bob's merciful spirit prompted him to accept.

At home, the news was received with interest. But two members of our household projected an immediate positive response: Alice and John. Alice selected one of the pictures of an orphan child and said, "I want her." And from that day till this she has faithfully given money to help "her child."

John's response was similar. He, too, selected a little Korean girl. The actions of these two young people were not surprising. Alice baby-sits for a one-and-a-half-year-old girl whose mother is gone much of the time. John was instantly attracted to Alwyn. He talks to her, picks her up, and cuddles her. Alwyn seeks out

John whenever she comes into the house. "John . . . John . . ." she says, running to his room and calling him. When John is there, he stops whatever he is doing and responds to her.

Perhaps one reason John responds to Alwyn so deeply is because of the little girl's need for security. His merciful nature is especially sensitive to feel a child's hunger for acceptance and act accordingly.

Another merciful person is my mother. She is one of the most gracious ladies I've ever known, and I've always admired her quiet, gentle ways. But during my growing-up years, I neither fully understood her nor the reasons why she and I so frequently seemed to be at cross purposes with one another. Today, with my present understanding of personal gifts—mine and hers in particular—I realize that those misunderstandings were not necessary. And they would not have existed if she and I had only understood our intrinsically different approaches to everything:

It was her nature to touch; mine to remain cool and aloof.

It was her nature to weep easily; mine to remain stoic.

It was her nature to overemphasize personal hurts and rebuffs; mine to underemphasize them.

It was her nature to sympathize with one's situation or condition; mine to project plans for changing one's situation.

She greatly enjoyed listening to an overtly emotional preacher or teacher; my enjoyment was to listen to a self-controlled, logical preacher or teacher.

She was sensitive to the atmosphere of a meeting or service; while I was sensitive to the planning and execution of the meeting or service.

She enjoyed an informal social interaction; while I preferred a more formal interaction.

Because my mother was a godly woman, she wanted her children to develop into God-honoring, God-fearing individuals. Therefore, my innate traits which were so different from hers—because of our differing personal gifts—caused my mother much trepidation. She feared that I was not developing into the godly woman she so desired me to be.

For example, she could not comprehend how a person could sit through a stirring gospel message without weeping. My apparent lack of sympathy seemed cold and unfeeling, very un-Christlike to her.

She humbles herself by esteeming others better than herself. Because of her strong inclination toward humility, she reacts to attitudes she considers prideful. She abhors a mocking or sarcastic attitude. Yet, because of her dread of any confronting situation, she will tolerate (outwardly acting in a pleasant manner) individuals or situations that wound her. My mother radiates sympathy, empathy, and compassion. Even her voice has a sympathetic tone. She is a good listener, in that she gives patient, sincere attention to whatever another person has to say.

Let me give some examples of merciful listeners who also give expected and needed empathetic responses.

Richard, who is eight, got a haircut from a new barber just two days before Thanksgiving Day. The barber clipped him very short, extremely short, in fact. He came home upset and angry. He accosted his father.

"Dad, I'm not going to the school Thanksgiving party looking like this!"

His father paused in his reading and eyed his son speculatively. "Why? Do you think your friends will make fun of you?"

Richard slammed his fist into his other palm. "I *know* they'll make fun of me. They'll tell me I look bald. Bald and silly."

His father answered kindly, "I can understand. I know it won't be easy to walk into the party looking like you do." Then suddenly he jumped up and began walking around his son, impersonating Richard's favorite comedian. As he scrutinized him, he asked in a low-pitched voice, "What happened to you? You look like you've been . . . like you've been scalped."

As he watched his father's antics, Richard relaxed, then

laughed, joining in the fun. "I'll just give a war whoop and say, 'The Indians did it!' Then they'll laugh with me, instead of laughing at me."

Richard's father, had he not acted in accordance with his gift of mercy, could have mismanaged the situation with such worn-out platitudes as: "So they'll laugh. Let them laugh! What do you care?" Or, "Just ignore them." Or, "You should have seen me when I went into the Army. They *shaved* me!"

None of this would have helped. But because he acknowledged his boy's predicament and validated his feeling, he was able to help him. By voicing Richard's anticipated embarrassment, and helping him to see the humor in the situation, he enabled his son to discover his own solution to the problem.

Three-year-old Billy was experiencing his first episode with a baby-sitter. When his parents left his sight, he began to cry very hard. Nothing Meagan could do helped. He would not eat. He would not play with his favorite toys. Nor would he go to sleep.

Finally Meagan empathized with him by making up a song. She held him and rocked him while singing, "Billy wishes his Mommy was here. Uh-huh. Billy wishes Daddy was here. Uh-huh. Billy wishes Daddy and Mommy were here. Uh-huh. . . ."

Suddenly Billy stopped crying. "Sing again," he said.

So Meagan repeated her made-up song several times. Billy listened intently. Then he sat up and smiled. "Let's play train."

He was perfectly happy the rest of the evening.

Both children and adults feel loved and understood when they are in the company of individuals with the personal gift of mercy, because their feelings are recognized as being authentic and valid.

However, because of his strong desire to empathize, the person with the personal gift of mercy may find it difficult to stand alone and tends to be easily influenced by others.

My nephew John gave me an illustration of this principle from his personal experience. He said that when he was in high school, he was one of the few kids who had a car. This, of course, made him popular, but it also presented some problems. Such as:

"John, let's cut class today," one of his friends said one afternoon. "Let's cut class and go to the beach."

"Naw, I want to go to school," John said.

"Go to school! Man, who wants to go to school? School's a drag. Let's go to the beach."

"Yeah," several others chimed in. "C'mon, John. We'll even pay your way."

"I've cut too many classes already," John said, "and I'm in trouble with my dad."

"What are you, John, chicken?"

"No, I'm not chicken. I just don't want to cut class today. That's what," John said, beginning to weaken with all the pressure.

"In the end, I often went with them," John said. " I *really* didn't want to go with them. But I did want to have friends. So I did what they wanted me to do."

The strong desire that accompanies the personal gift of mercy also often expresses itself in special kinds of compassion. In my book *The Idea Book for Mothers* (Tyndale House, 1981), I mentioned a person with this gift. His name was Jeff. I can never forget him. He loved animals and birds and responded to their traumas as though they were his very own.

Everybody in the neighborhood knew Jeff. He was always mending a bird's broken wing, or nursing a stray dog. Often when I looked out my window, I would see Jeff slipping a jar lid of milk out by the garage for some sickly cat. But his compassion also extended to people: he would reach out to unfortunate boys or girls and help them, encourage them. He became arms for those who were without, and legs for those who had none. Jeff, with his personal gift of mercy, was loved by all who knew him for his quiet, gentle, caring ways.

This same desire to protect the helpless, especially animals, was also a part of Alice's innate nature. She loved animals, too, and they loved and trusted her. Alice is my fourth child, my second daughter. She was a physically beautiful child from birth. And even as a baby, she reached out to touch and love both people and animals. She enjoyed being touched and fondled, and was easily wounded by even an unintentional slight. But she was also inclined to exaggerate emotional hurts and to blow them out of proportion.

Alice was very sensitive to words and actions that would hurt or offend. She became the champion of the underdog, the down-trodden, the minority. She would stand up for them and come to their aid. This trait became apparent during her elementary school years.

During those years we lived in a rural section of Michigan and many of our neighbors were Amish. Because they were distinct-ly in the minority, and lived and dressed differently from most of the other children, they were the frequent butt of slights and jeers. Alice identified with them. She went to their aid. She made friends with the Amish children, chose them to be on her team for games, and invited them to her house to play.

Individuals with the personal gift of mercy also tend to be very protective, especially of family and friends.

Keith, who is my middle son, has exuded gentleness and compassion from the time he was a toddler. He has always been a peacemaker. And since Keith is the middle child of five chil-dren, he was afforded much opportunity for peacemaking. He was always willing to defer to the desires or tastes of others— for the sake of peace. And from a very early age he has reached out to remove hurts from others.

When Keith was about two, his same-age cousin came to spend the day. It was Shelly's first time alone at our house, and as soon as my brother drove off, she began crying.

THE MERCY STYLE OF PARENTING

Terry and Trish said, "Be quiet, Shelly."

But Shelly wouldn't stop crying.

Keith watched the situation for a few minutes, then quietly left the room. Wondering what he would do, I followed him. Keith trotted over to where his Uncle Randall had left Shelly's things. He dug around until he found Shelly's "special" blanket.

He hurried back and handed her the blanket. Then he sat down beside his distraught cousin and patted her comfortingly.

Keith has always been especially protective of me, quick to come to my aid or support in any situation. He was also the first to assist me when I had many things to do, or to ease any pressure that was coming against me. As a teenager he assumed a special responsibility for me and his younger sister and brother for several years. Even when he was away at college, he assisted us financially from the meager monies that he earned, ever wanting to protect me from any lack or hurt.

A couple of weeks ago I had the pleasurable opportunity of viewing a videotape of Keith's television show. The format consists of a thirty-minute interview, followed by thirty minutes of preaching. I was deeply moved as my middle son effectively communicated via the TV screen.

As he ministered, I was aware of his personal gift of mercy in a new way. His caring countenance, his sincere sensitivity to those to whom he was directing his message came through. His total being projected his loving belief that the viewers could receive God's deliverance from whatever had them in bondage.

If I were to give a one-sentence descriptive comparison of my three sons, as viewed by their school peers, I would say: Terry was held in awe for his knowledge and erudition. David strongly attracted or repelled others because of his imaginative and unconventional ideas. And Keith was loved for his empathy.

Though there is great warmth and power for healing in the one with the personal gift of mercy, the gentle nature of such people may make it difficult for them to withstand stress or personal attack. And if those stresses or attacks are prolonged or often repeated, they will inevitably result in depression, physical difficulties, or a resigned martyr complex.

Such people also find it painful to make difficult decisions; and because of decision-procrastination, the person with the personal gift of mercy often allows the pressures of time or events to make decisions for him.

A red flag for the mercy-giver to be aware of is that the personal tendency to avoid firmness or confrontation may result in a pattern of inconsistency or indecisiveness.

That's exactly the position Christopher found himself in. As a man with the personal gift of mercy, he tended to be inconsistent in abiding by his decisions. However, he soon discovered that this trait mitigated against him with his emotionally unstable wife. Even when Christopher was firm with her, she had learned that her constant, negative pressure would usually wear him down.

When Christopher came home one day and informed his wife that they were invited to a company banquet, she was upset.

"Let's not go," she pleaded. "Those meetings bore me."

"It's important to me . . . to us . . . that we go," he said. "As an executive, I'm expected to be there."

With that, tears rolled down Ruth's cheeks. "You never think of me, or what's important to me."

"That's not true," Christopher said. "Since I know you don't like to go to these functions, I rarely ask you to go. But this is a very important banquet, and I'm expected to be there."

"Well, we'll see," she said.

The afternoon of the banquet, Ruth was in bed with "a splitting headache" when Christopher arrived home. "If you're going to your banquet, you'll have to find someone to watch the children, I can't," she sobbed.

Christopher stood looking at her for a long moment, then sighed. "OK, Ruth . . . I won't go." He turned tiredly away and softly closed the door.

Another caution area is the mercy-giver's intense desire to empathize and to soothe hurts, which sometimes traps him into feeding another's self-pity.

Kevin and Eileen had been married for seven years and had three children, the oldest five and the youngest three months. Kevin was the traveling representative for a new computer company and his work took him away from home much of the time. He loved his family and was with them constantly when he was home. But Eileen was beginning to resent his frequent absences. She confided this to her long-time friend, Carolyn.

"The children sometimes wonder if they have a daddy," Eileen said. "And I'm getting to hate to see him packing."

"You poor dear," Carolyn sympathized. "It must be awful."

Eileen dabbed at her eyes. "It *is* awful. Just awful. . . ."

Carolyn put her arm around her friend's shoulder and patted her like she would a child. "Does Kevin know how you feel?"

"Yes . . . but he says he has to go." She wept.

"I just know how lonesome you get," Carolyn said, "and how *hard* it must be, with the children to care for and all. . . ."

"I don't know what I'm going to do . . . I just don't know."

Carolyn massaged her friend's shoulders. "I understand, Eileen. You're so brave to tolerate such a difficult life."

All throughout this chapter, we have looked at people of all ages who possess the personal gift of mercy. Some of the professions that may be suited to these people in a special way are: musician, actor, poet, doctor (all healing ministries), artist, foster home director, and veterinarian.

As you examine the following list of characteristics for those with the personal gift of mercy, keep this basic principle in mind: As with the previous six personal gifts, you must carefully separate learned skills and professions from traits that are intrinsically yours—remembering that the traits of your personal gift bring joy in your approach to any situation.

For example: Miriam is the superintendent of Happy Acres, a halfway house for handicapped children. All of the patients have undergone treatment at the hospital and are spending time at Happy Acres, learning how to cope with either a home or "real-life" situation before being discharged.

Because her situation is so obviously a ministry of comfort and healing, Miriam is viewed by her friends and associates as one gifted with the personal gift of mercy. But this is not the case. Miriam has *learned* how to deal kindly with these handicapped children in ways to which they respond. However, Miriam's personal gift of administration means that her great joy comes from the planning, organizing, and setting of goals for each child, as well as from the running of Happy Acres itself.

So, again, how easily one's personal gift was confused with or misconstrued from a learned skill or profession. Be sure to keep this in mind as you study the following list.

Style Guide for the Personal Gift of Mercy

1. Has a special ability to identify with those in distress, coupled with the capacity to remove hurts and bring comfort.
2. Shows sensitivity in looking at things from the viewpoint of others.
3. Tends to be an empathetic listener.
4. At times may feed another's self-pity by his extreme empathy.
5. Is able to yield his personal rights and expectations.
6. Tends to be easily hurt.
7. Is sensitive to actions and words that will hurt or offend others. His voice may even carry a sympathetic tone to it.
8. Desires to support and protect.
9. Behaves in a humble manner and strongly reacts to pride.
10. Finds it difficult to withstand stress and personal attack.
11. Reacts to people who seem to be callous, indifferent, or given to partiality.
12. May tend to be guided by his emotions, and may therefore appear undisciplined.
13. Likes to be around people and enjoys social interaction (when not depressed or feeling like a martyr).
14. Weeps easily.
15. Lack of overt firmness may appear to be indecisiveness.
16. Strongly desires harmony to the degree that he may compromise for peace.
17. His avoidance of confrontation may be interpreted as weakness.
18. Tends to use body language and is sensitive to the body language of others.

FAMILY INFLUENCE ON PERSONAL GIFTS

"I am seeking for my gift," the young man said.

"Does everybody have a personal gift?" I was asked.

"Help me find my gift," the young woman implored me.

"I don't think I have a *personal* gift," an older adult said.

"I think I have a gift . . . that is, I believe God must have given me one," another person said, "but I'm not at all certain what it is."

This is just a sampling of the many, many comments and questions I hear about this matter of personal gifts. Confusion about "whether I have one or not," or, "maybe God doesn't want everyone to have one . . ." And on and on.

So, once again I will reiterate: my understanding of personal gifts is that they are innate. That is, God has given a personal gift to each child at birth. And this personal gift tempers and determines the approach each child takes (or will take) to everything in life. This gift is *not* hereditary in nature, because genetics have nothing to do with it.

However, what a child *does* with his personal gift will largely depend upon the example or model his parents or other significant persons provide for him. Each child can and will, I believe, choose to accept and develop, or reject and nullify his personal gift.

If the child accepts his personal gift, he will allow it to grow, to develop and blossom into the beautiful, full-blown creation that God intended. If the child chooses to reject his gift, it will become stultified, or stunted, and may shrivel until it becomes a barely recognizable vestige of what it was intended to be.

If the child chooses to reject his gift, he will do so in one of three ways: (1) by *submerging* it, (2) by *sublimating* it, or (3) by *perverting* it. Let's look at these three one at a time.

A person *submerges* his personal gift if he *consciously* attempts to emphasize a different personal gift than the one God has given him. He *sublimates* his personal gift if he *subconsciously* attempts to emphasize a different personal gift than the one God has given him. And he *perverts* his personal gift if he attempts to emphasize opposite (or negative) characteristics of the ones peculiar to his God-given personal gift (*or* if he refuses to allow God to be glorified through or by his gift). These perversions can take place in varying degrees of consciousness.

Every child has an especially significant person in his life. *Significant:* the word connotes important or meaningful. For a newborn baby, the most important, most meaningful person in his life is the one who provides him with his necessities, his constant care. In our society this is usually the mother or the father. However, it isn't long—a few years at the most—until the child determines for himself which person or persons he believes are the most important or significant to his life.

This significant person(s) upon whom he focuses will greatly affect the emergence or the submergence of his personal gift, which will depend upon whether the child admires and respects him or whether the opposite is true. In either case the child's attitude toward that significant person will largely determine either the emergence or the stultification of his personal gift. For example:

PRINCIPLE NUMBER ONE

If the significant person has a *different* personal gift than the child, and the child admires or respects him, then the child may reject his own personal gift *in order to emulate that significant person.*

Some of my own children serve to illustrate this principle. Keith, for instance, rejected his personal gift of mercy by *submerging* it. Since I was the significant person in Keith's life, and he admired me very much, he chose to model himself after me. In order to do this, he attempted to emulate my personal gift (which is ruling/administration).

This was not easily done. Keith's natural gift of mercy dictated that he react or respond to situations emotionally; whereas I tend not to be overtly governed or directed by emotional stimuli. So throughout most of his growing-up years Keith was embarrassed by this natural tendency of his. This was partially because he so desired to be like me, and partially because of the totality of his milieu, which decreed that "Boys are sissies if they show emotions, and/or if they don't participate in rugged, he-man sports."

Since Keith's tendency *was* to be governed by emotions, and since he *didn't* enjoy football and other rough sports, he came to view his personal gift (which he didn't then understand) as a weakness.

Therefore, he consciously strove to hide his emotions and his emotional approach to situations, and tried to develop the crisp, business-organizational approach which characterized me. He did this to become as much like me as possible.

Today Keith is a grown man who works with an international Christian humanitarian organization, which involves dealing with or ministering to those who are hurting or in need. Now he understands his personal gift and is allowing his merciful approach to reach out in caring ways to all he comes in contact with.

But how much better it would have been for Keith and me if I had recognized our personal gifts years ago! I could then have helped him develop his gift by teaching him how to understand it. He could then have more effectively stood against the forces that mitigated against his God-given gift of mercy.

In chapter 7, I gave the illustration of my daughter Trish, who was viewed as having the same personal gift of administration as mine. This was because she had studied me and had learned her administrative skills by watching me. Trish did not *consciously* reject her personal gift of giving. However, she subconsciously did so, because the totality of her early environment stultified her own personal gift; which remained dormant for many years. So she *sublimated* her innate tendencies and modeled my approach to life situations.

PRINCIPLE NUMBER TWO

Another method of rejecting one's personal gift is by perversion. This often results from the child's frustration with the significant person whom he admires.

My youngest daughter, Alice, will serve as an illustration of this principle. In retrospect, I can now see that I often frustrated Alice while she was yet a tiny child, because I didn't touch or cuddle her as much as she desired or needed. Neither did I overtly respond to people, situations, *or* to her beloved animals. And there were many times when I was quite stern with her because of her emotional and frequently indecisive approach.

Because I understood neither my personal gift nor hers, I became frustrated with her when she didn't approach situations as I did. I believed that the best thing I could do for her was try to help her become more like me. I was unaware of the devastating power that my words possessed to wound Alice's sensitive spirit. Nor could I understand that her increasingly emotional responses and indecisive actions were often aimed at "getting back" at me.

But since Alíce did admire me, and because our differing personal gifts made it impossible for her to be just like me, she often felt unworthy or inadequate. This, of course, affected the development of her self-esteem. As a result, Alíce also at times rejected her mercy approach by emphasizing the negative or red flag aspects of her personal gift of mercy.

But now, since Alíce and I both understand our individual personal gifts, Alíce has greater freedom to become the sweet, sensitive person God intended her to be. We have both learned that it's all right for the two of us to be different, and to approach things differently, as long as we both move in obedience to the Word of God.

PRINCIPLE NUMBER THREE

If a child does *not* admire the significant person in his life, *and the two possess different personal gifts,* then the child will probably accept his personal gift; and he may choose to enhance that gift, *in order to use it as a means of rebellion* against that significant person.

Professor Berne, a friend of mine, who was chairman of the Division of Psychology in a midwestern college, will serve as an illustration of this precept. I now realize that Professor Berne had the personal gift of teaching, while his son has the personal gift of ministry. The professor hoped that his son would follow in his footsteps and become a learned and educated man; but it seemed that everything he did drove this possibility further and further from him. Throughout most of the years the boy was growing up, his father was always studying and earning more degrees. Then when his father became a full professor he was surrounded by a cortege of students.

Barrett grew to resent his father's frequent absences, then his preoccupation with students; so he resentfully refused to study and spent his time tinkering with cars. The conflict between the two continued and the chasm widened, resulting in great strife in the home.

But even though Barrett persistently developed the "physical-ness" of his personal gift of ministry to spite his father, it benefited him personally, and he eventually became the owner of a successful auto body shop. However, this mutual lack of understanding eventuated in a parting of their ways.

We have been discussing children who possess personal gifts which *differ* from those of their parents and/or significant persons in their lives. Now I am turning my attention to the children having the *same* personal gift as the significant parent or person in their lives.

PRINCIPLE NUMBER FOUR

When a child possesses the *same* personal gift as the significant person in his life, and admires and respects him, the result is the full blossoming of the child's gift, which enables him to enjoy the gracious gift of joy it was meant to be.

An example of the above has to do with a friend of my husband Bob. A well-known speaker and writer, he and his son possess the personal gift of exhorting. From a tiny child, the boy modeled himself after his father. And even though the father was often gone on speaking trips, the boy never evidenced resentment. Across the years, the two have become good friends and are a source of mutual enrichment and encouragement to each other.

Since the son had a godly model who constantly developed and enjoyed his own personal gift, the son did the same. Thus he had always been able to grow and blossom, becoming all that God intended him to be. Today, they serve God together, speaking and counseling in an almost identical manner in their own evangelistic counseling center.

PRINCIPLE NUMBER FIVE

When a child possesses the *same* personal gift as the significant person in his life, but *does not* admire and respect him, the child is likely to reject his own personal gift.

Let me give examples of two different methods of perversion: A college Bible professor told me this tragic story which illustrates how a child can *pervert his personal gift by rejecting God*. Both Professor Phillips and his son possess the personal gift of teaching. The father longed for his son to emulate him and become a Bible teacher. But to fulfill this great longing, Phillips wrongly used his influence to close other avenues of study which interested his son. This produced such a high frustration level in the boy that he rejected both his father and his father's God. He left home, went to India, and became a guru.

Sally, who was in my son David's Sunday school, also illustrates the above principle. Both Sally and her mother possessed the personal gift of mercy. Sally viewed her mother as a weak person when she brought an ungodly stepfather into the home, and grew to resent her. As a result, Sally rejected and perverted her merciful approach.

Since Sally was too young to leave home, she was forced to live in that hostile environment for several years. The results were devastating. Sally consciously submerged her positive qualities and overtly acted out the negative (or opposite) traits of her personal gift. And during the times when Sally felt herself emotionally drawn toward those who were hurting, the extreme perversion of her gift caused her to re-focus on her own trauma. Then she would try to make others hurt as badly as she did.

To make matters worse, during the infrequent periods of comparative serenity at home, Sally initiated disturbances. She continuously expressed her negative emotions, antagonized people, and then withdrew into herself. Everybody then disliked her even more, which "justified" Sally's growing martyr complex.

Sally's very presence exuded negativism and depression, and her life became a totally joyless existence.

What an ironical paradox!

God provided each of us with our very own personal gift, our charisma, which is to be our "gracious gift of joy." And it is this personal gift which is the *very key* to the full development of our personalities. Acceptance and development of this personal gift inevitably brings joy. Rejection and perversion of this gift inevitably results in apathy and despair.

A Holy Spirit-ruled person—one who is motivated and moved by his gracious personal gift—will radiate joy. What dynamism is released by that personal gift! When that God-bestowed gift is accepted, understood, and allowed to blossom and develop, it becomes more than a gift. It also becomes a tool through which we can in turn bestow God's love upon others.

This received and developed gift is the synergism which provides wholeness to a person. It is the released "atomic power" that enables families to function harmoniously. That is why it is so important for parents to understand their own gift and those of their children, then teach their children how to sensitively approach life situations as their personal gifts direct. Such informed and Spirit-directed parents will not attempt to force their children to approach life as they do (if their personal gifts happen to differ).

As you are in the process of discovering and developing your personal gift (yours and your children's), let me suggest several concepts it will be helpful to remember.

1. A clear understanding of personal gifts makes it possible for *every parent* and *every child* to realize his full personal and familial potential. This is particularly true when each one is living in complete harmony and obedience to God's Word.

2. Remember, a personal gift does not necessarily limit one's choice of a profession. A person with any one of the seven personal gifts named in Romans 12:6-8 can choose any profession. The professions listed with each of chapters 2 through 8 merely indicate a "tendency toward." But there are many variables, many extenuating circumstances that could affect each person's environment and selection of a profession or occupation. For example, the chapter on the personal gift of exhorting did not list administration as one possible profession. Yet my friend Nancy, who has the personal gift of exhorting, is an outstanding administrator. It is just that some professions may be more conducive to the joy-flow of a personal gift than another.

3. Personal gifts are not inherited. To think that they are is to

allow room for tragic misunderstandings. In many homes where a child has approached everything differently than his parents (whether biological or adoptive), the child has been taken from one doctor or psychologist to another in an attempt to determine, "What's wrong with my child?" When, in reality, there's nothing wrong with either the parent or the child. The problem is simply in the misunderstanding of the parent's and the child's personal gift.

4. It must be kept in mind that the personal gifts, the *charismata* listed in Romans 12:6-8, are the specific gifts which are being discussed within the parameters of this book. However, this grouping is in no way intended to describe the extent of God's gifts to his creatures. For his gifts include his Son, Jesus Christ, salvation, his revealed Word, grace, his love, and many, many others. James attempts to describe the extent of God's gifts when he says, "Every good gift and every perfect gift is from above, and cometh down from the Father" (James 1:17). But the scope of this book is focused on the personal gifts as given to individuals.

So I ask again the questions that are often voiced:

"How can one find and utilize *his* personal gifts?"

"How can one help his family find *their* personal gifts?"

Read or reread chapters 2 through 8. As you do so, open yourself up to the Holy Spirit. Ask him to come into your life, to fill you, to empower you, to excite you, to reproduce his joy in you. Then consciously seek his leading—through the constant filling of yourself with God's Word.

By so doing, not just once, but continuously, by daily making yourself available to be used by him in every way, you will find yourself joyously looking forward to each new day—because each new day will be filled again with new joy.

As you reread chapters 2 through 8, please heed the caution that I have added to each one of those chapters, which is to take time to meditate, to pray, and to carefully be led into your decision as to which of the personal gifts is yours or your child's.

Then when you isolate your personal gift . . . and when you

live your life filled with the joy it brings, you will find yourself alive in new ways. And the joy you exude will influence others to seek and appropriate the joy that you and your family have found.

PERSONAL GIFTS FROM FAMILY PERSPECTIVES

It was a rainy afternoon and David was slightly chilled when he walked in from his afternoon college classes. Bob and I were seated before the fireplace, clipboards in hand. I had just prepared us both a cup of herbal tea which we were sipping as we worked.

David moved to the blazing fire to warm himself. "Mmmm," he said, "it smells good. I think I'd like a cup."

I looked up from my work. "The water's hot," I said. "The tea and honey are near the stove. The mugs are in the cupboard. Help yourself." And I continued working.

Bob paused. "Dave, go change your wet clothes and I'll have a cup for you by the time you're ready."

David grinned good-naturedly. "It's a good thing I know each of my parent's personal gift."

"Why's that?" I asked.

He grinned again. "Well . . . otherwise I might think my mother wasn't showing Christian love. Or else, she was angry at me." He chuckled, then ducked into his bedroom. Bob got up and prepared David's tea.

In every family, at some time or another, the difference in the various members' personal gifts could give rise to misunderstandings. However, when each knows not just his own personal gift, but the gifts of his siblings and parents, much potential cause for irritation can be minimized or eliminated. The following illustration will clarify this principle.

In the Perry Anderson family there are six children. Including Louise (the mother), all seven of the gifts are represented, but *two* of the family members possess *the same personal gift*. In this particular incident, Aaron (whose personal gift is ministry—the same as his oldest sister, Jennifer), had an important decision to make. He shared it with his family one Sunday afternoon. The results are very revealing, and I believe most of us can identify to some degree with one or another of the individuals involved.

The dessert had just been served and for the moment nobody was talking. Aaron nervously cleared his throat. "I'd like all of your advice on something," he said. He said it in such a manner that everybody paused and looked at him.

Aaron took a deep breath. "I saw somebody take something at school . . . and I want you to help me decide what to do. Friday, after I'd left PE, I noticed I'd forgotten and left my watch in my locker. So I went back. And that's when I saw it happen."

"Saw what happen?" Camile asked rather impatiently.

"The coach wasn't in the PE office when I got there. But just as I walked in the door, I saw Joel Foster open the cash box. That's where the coach keeps our intra-mural money. And he took out a handful of bills."

"Did Joel see you?" Aaron's mother asked.

Aaron shook his head. "No. I ducked back in the hallway and went back to my class without my watch. Now I'm not sure what to do about it."

PERSONAL GIFTS FROM FAMILY PERSPECTIVES

Camile spoke sternly (her personal gift is prophecy), "I think you should go right to the coach and tell him what you saw. The boy stole something that didn't belong to him. He should have to pay."

Marjorie started to cry (her personal gift is mercy). "Joel is in my history class," she said when she could get the words out. "His mother's sick and his father's drunk most of the time. I think you shouldn't do anything."

Mrs. Anderson (whose personal gift is giving) put her hand on her husband's arm. "Perry, we have the bonus money you received last week. Let's just let Aaron give it to them."

Perry shook his head (his personal gift is administration/ruling). "Louise, I think it would be better to plan not only for this need but also for the future. I believe Aaron should first tell Joel that he saw him take the money. Then he can tell Joel that I can find him a job down at the plant next summer. That way Joel can earn enough money to pay back what he took, plus save a little for his needs the following year."

James (whose personal gift is exhorting) had been playing with his dessert spoon. Now he spoke up. "Why don't you talk to Joel and get his side of the story. Try to be his friend. Maybe there are some extenuating circumstances. . . ."

"For stealing?" Camile said. "I think Aaron should turn him in."

William, the youngest of the family (whose personal gift is teaching) said, "I think somebody should teach Joel that it's wrong to steal." He looked around the table. "Maybe he doesn't know it's wrong. I don't think he goes to church anywhere." William went on. "Aaron could tell him about God and how to live by God's words. I think that's what he should do."

Jennifer (whose personal gift is ministry) spoke last. "Well, I think Aaron should go over to Joel's house and help him do whatever his family needs to have done. You should *show* him that somebody cares about him."

Mr. Anderson looked at Aaron. "Well, son, we've all given you our own perspective. Now, it's up to you. What are you going to do?"

Aaron's face was very serious. "I appreciate what all of you have said. But I think Jennifer is right. Tomorrow I'll go and help him work around his house. Then I'll ask him if he'll help me with lawn jobs during spring vacation next week. He could make quite a bit of money to help him out right now."

Can you see what happened here? Each person counseled Aaron from the point of view of his or her own personal gift. And interestingly enough, even though he had asked for advice, Aaron found all of their advice unacceptable except for Jennifer's—because none of the other advisors spoke from a point of view that matched his approach to doing things. It wasn't that one person's advice was right and the others' were wrong, but that Aaron could best follow the advice of the person whose personal gift was the same as his own.

When a person receives counsel or advice from one whose personal gift *is different from his own,* he may be unable to follow through on it. The reason is that, for him, the advice might be confusing, frustrating, or even wrong.

Furthermore, if a parent who does not know his own personal gift, or that of his child, were to advise or even urge his child to act as he would in a situation, the child would be unable to joyfully follow through. He might even be unable to follow through at all. However, if the child attempted to follow the advice given him, the following results could occur:

(1) If the child was unable to successfully carry out his parent's directions, he would consider himself to have failed.

(2) Then, because he had "failed," the child would probably feel guilty, inadequate, and therefore under condemnation.

(3) Because of his "failure" to accomplish his parent's commands, the child might become resentful toward his parent.

Let me give an illustration which clarifies this principle:

Neal and his oldest son, Jerome, possess the personal gift of giving; while Glenn, the younger son's personal gift is administration.

When Neal returned home one evening, he found his teenage

sons in an unusually jubilant mood. They met him at the door, waving envelopes. "Hi, Dad," Glenn said. "Our income tax refunds came today. Here's yours."

"That's great!" Neal said, ripping open the envelope. He grinned when he showed them the amount. Dinner was especially upbeat that evening. Afterward the boys followed their father into the family room, while their mother retired to the living room to read.

Neal leaned back in his comfortable chair while Glenn lit a fire in the fireplace. "Boys," Neal began, "I suggest we pool our income tax refunds, put the money to work for the Lord. I know just the place for it."

Jerome sat up straight. "Where's that, Dad?"

"Remember your Uncle Bill's last prayer letter from Uganda? Well, he said they urgently need a small printing press. And I believe . . . by putting our money together, we can buy it for him. What do you think of that idea?"

Glenn concentrated on stoking and didn't answer. Jerome spoke enthusiastically, "Good old Uncle Bill. Dad, I like that idea. I'm all for it." He turned toward his silent younger brother. "What about you, Glenn?"

Glenn didn't speak immediately. He ran his fingers through his hair and took a deep breath. "Dad," he began, "I thought . . . well, I want to save this money."

Jerome's face showed his incredulity. "You mean you *don't want to give* to Uncle Bill?"

Glenn went on as though he hadn't heard. ". . . I've been saving to go to Westmont College . . . and, well, I *did* tithe my money when I earned it. Well, I thought I'd put this money in the bank with my college fund."

"That's selfish," Jerome burst out. "Uncle Bill *needs* that printing press. Now! Your college is two years away!"

"I know that, Jerome. But . . . well, I'm also planning ahead for law school."

Neal spoke slowly. "Of course, Glenn, *it is* your money. And I realize that giving to God's work is a privilege, not a duty."

There was a long, uncomfortable silence. Then Jerome turned his back toward Glenn and asked his father about proceeding with their gift. The two of them began discussing the printing press. Glenn left the room in confusion. He had thought that the Holy Spirit had been directing his life plans. But now he felt guilty and condemned by his father and brother. It seemed that they were *always* giving.

Something must be wrong with him . . . maybe he was selfish. . . .

You can readily see that, for Glenn, all three parts of the previously stated principle apply to him. He was unable to do as his father suggested, which brought guilt and condemnation, which could ultimately result in resentment. Furthermore, because neither the father nor his sons understands his own individual personal gift, future counseling or illustrative situations are not likely to conclude any differently than this one did. And so the guilt and resentment begin to compound.

This is why great wisdom needs to be exercised in group advice (such as a parent to all his children, a teacher to his total class, a pastor to his whole congregation), for unless the advisor understands all seven of the personal gifts, the results of such general advice could be confusion, condemnation, and resentment.

By now you are realizing the importance of parents knowing both their own personal gifts and those of their children. Because only then can they understand their children's point of view, and why they approach life situations differently than they themselves do. Such understanding brings great clarity and strength to the advice a parent gives.

For example: Byron has taken a two-month leave of absence from his work to run a youth camp for his church. He has done this for the past several years, but this year for the first time he has enlisted the aid of his teenage son and daughter as counsel-

ors to the junior-age children. Both Byron and sixteen-year-old
Stacy possess the personal gift of ministry; while fifteen-year-old
Bret possesses the personal gift of teaching.

In conference with his new youth counselors, Byron advises,
"Remember, we are here to serve the kids. Keep that in mind.
And whether you are leading them on an overnight, or superin-
tending their swimming activities, *show them* how to do what-
ever activity you are engaged in. Remember that: show them.
Got it?"

While instructing his young counselors, Byron forgot for the
moment that his two children's personal gifts differed, though his
and his daughter's were the same. He was reminded of this one
day as he was making his rounds. When he reached the pool
area, instead of hearing and seeing the children in the water, he
saw them clustered around Bret.

And to his utter astonishment, he heard his son giving a
lecture on human anatomy. "Look at this chart," Bret was saying.
"These are the muscles of the body. And these large ones here
. . . and here . . . they are the ones you use when you are
swimming. Now, it's important that you know how they operate
. . . because when you are rescuing someone from drowning. . . ."

Byron was upset. He had engaged his son to demonstrate
lifesaving methods—but not to teach a pre-med course in anatomy. Later he called his son aside. "Look, Bret," he began, "I heard
your lecture by the pool today."

Bret grinned. "They liked it, Dad. Tomorrow I'm going to. . . ."

Byron interrupted. "No, Bret. Just *show them* how to rescue
someone from the water. And show how to provide artificial
respiration. That's all. They don't need all that other."

Bret broke in. "Wait a minute, Dad. Please listen. I know that
you want to benefit the kids here. . . . I mean you want to help
them *physically do things.* I know that. But I want to go beyond
just showing them what to do in the water. I want to give them
the *why* of things. I think that's important for them to know."

All at once Byron saw his error. Bret was right. It wasn't that his son didn't want to follow his instructions. It was just that he'd always approached everything like he was doing right now—defining and explaining things.

Byron took a deep breath. "I'm sorry, son. I spoke too hastily. You're right. And you're doing a great job. It's different from the way I would do it. But that doesn't matter. You do it best your way . . . and your joy is contagious. Keep it up."

He gave his son a friendly slap on the shoulder. "You tell 'em, son. And I'll show them."

Because Byron knew his personal gift and his son's, he was able to allow his son to be himself. And he didn't attempt to force his son to do things the way he would have.

When parents are able to coordinate and harmonize the responses of each family member, they will be able to help realize the full potential of each.

And if each practicing Christian properly understood his personal gift, the whole Body of Christ would benefit. It would not, as some may think, give license to attitudes of "this is the way I am and I can't help how I am." Rather, understanding personal gifts helps to: (1) clarify those individual attributes that complement and edify the Body of Christ; (2) bring an awareness of those individual attributes that could be a stumbling block in the Body of Christ (unless there is a daily commitment to being led by the Holy Spirit).

When a parent (or anyone) makes such a commitment, then he will be motivated and empowered to greater service. Corporately, such commitment among family members and individuals-at-large would result in a new wave of excitement and power to the Body of Christ.

And to that my friend Lisa would say, "Glory!"

ELEVEN

THERE IS A FUNCTION FOR EVERYONE

"I realize that I've got a personal gift," I often hear, "but what good is it? I don't seem to 'fit' anywhere."

"I'm not an apostle," a young man told my husband, "And I'm definitely not a prophet . . . or an evangelist, either, for that matter . . . I really don't know what I'm supposed to do."

One rather harried young woman said, "I've been slotted to teach a class of junior-age girls . . . and I've been trying to teach them. But I know *and they know* that it's just not working. So what do I do now?"

Maybe you have asked questions like these yourself. Or you might have asked some even more basic ones. Such as, "I know what my gift is. And I know I'm supposed to be a part of the Body . . . but what part am I? I don't know how to find out."

Young mothers frequently ask, "I am concerned about my place in the Body. But I'm also concerned about my children. *What about my children?* Are they supposed to function in the Body? And if they are, how and where are they to do so?"

These are some of the questions that come to me as I talk to people about personal gifts. They are all good questions—logical, basic questions that need to be answered. So the intent of this chapter is to help you answer those questions.

Our creative God is so precise and mathematical that he has personally seen to it that his Body has been provided with all the parts necessary to accomplish the task he has set before it.

In addition to giving us the individual personal gifts listed in Romans 12, God has set a variety of functions (offices or ministries) within his Body. These functions are listed in Ephesians 4:11 and 1 Corinthians 12:28, 29. Following is a list of these functions with a brief definition of each. The basis I used for these delineations was furnished by Dr. Hugh Ross, associate pastor of the Sierra Madre Congregational Church.

Apostles: the function of elders with a clear mandate from God, acknowledged as such by the other elders, to communicate through teaching and instruction the messages of God to those who have not yet heard these messages, and in so doing to oversee the establishing of new congregations of believers. (In today's society the term missionary is frequently used for those who fit this biblical pattern.)

Prophets: the function of elders with a clear mandate from God, acknowledged as such by the other elders, to declare primarily the purpose and ways of God, his salvation and his kingdom.

Evangelists: the function of elders with a clear mandate from God, acknowledged as such by the other elders, to declare the good news of salvation through Jesus Christ.

Pastors: the function of elders with a clear mandate from God, acknowledged as such by the other elders, to shepherd and care for the needs of specific groups of believers placed under their stewardship.

Teachers: the function of elders with a clear mandate from God, acknowledged as such by the other elders, to clarify and protect biblical truths by teaching and instructing others through didactic discourses the things of God and the responsibilities of men to God and others.

Miracles: the function of leaders with a clear mandate from God, acknowledged as such by the elders, to perform by the power of the Holy Spirit physical and/or spiritual deeds that in themselves are a supernatural demonstration of the power of God by which the laws of nature are altered, suspended, or controlled.

Gifts of healings: the function of leaders with a clear mandate from God, acknowledged as such by the elders, to administer physical and mental/emotional health and cures by the direction of the Holy Spirit.

Helps: the function of all believers not called to serve in another function, in the ministry of rendering assistance; *or* the function of a leader with a clear mandate from God, acknowledged as such by the elders, to oversee the ministry of rendering assistance within the Body of believers and to train all believers (not called to serve in another function) in the ministry of rendering assistance.

Governments: the function of leaders with a clear mandate from God, acknowledged as such by the elders, to guide, coordinate, and integrate the affairs and the ministries of the Body of believers, to oversee the ministry of administration.

Diversities of tongues: the function of leaders with a clear mandate from God, acknowledged as such by the elders, to speak by the power of the Holy Spirit in other languages, both of men and of angels, and/or to interpret these languages for the benefit of the Body of believers.

All of these ten functions are *ministry gifts to the church,* but the first five as listed in Ephesians 4:11 have been given primarily to edify the Body of Christ *by a consistent speaking out of the Word of God.* The additional five functions delineated in 1 Corinthians 12: 28, 29 (along with the restatement of three of the five named in Ephesians 4:11) are ministry gifts that *build and edify the Body in many ways.*

CHART ONE

Ephesians 4:11	Evangelists	
	Pastors	
	Apostles	
	Prophets	
	Teachers	
	Miracles	*1 Corinthians 12:28, 29*
	Gifts of healings	
	Helps	
	Governments	
	Diversities of tongues	

Every individual who receives Jesus as his Savior becomes *at that moment* a member of the Body of Christ, and as such, is also given (or called to) a function through which he is to magnify and glorify God. "For the body is not one member, but many. . . . But now hath God set the members every one of them in the body, as it hath pleased him" (1 Corinthians 12:14, 18).

Newborns in Christ are spiritual babies. And if they are also children, then they are babies physically as well. So the question arises, "Where could a *baby* function?"

I believe that every newborn child of God (regardless of age) will *first function in "helps."* The five ministry gifts listed in Ephesians 4:11 have been given to set the spiritual climate of the Body of Christ, so these must be filled by elders (those who are mature in the Word of God). Four of the additional five ministry gifts or functions listed in 1 Corinthians 12:28, 29 are also leadership functions and are best filled by spiritually mature believers.

However, *the function of helps is twofold:* general and leadership. The first part, or general function, includes the many-faceted area of rendering assistance; whereas, the second part is a called or "set apart" function in helps. It is in the general function of helps that a person's faithfulness will be established. And then God will speak and the sphere of the faithful one's service is enlarged and expanded. Only in rare instances does God call or indicate to a person that he is to serve in any leadership role in the Body of Christ until after he has served in the general function of helps. So until that time, God expects—he *requires*—faithfulness of us all (1 Corinthians 4:2).

For in our faithfulness we project to the world the faithfulness of God. And as we (every believer) render assistance, giving a cup of cold water in Jesus' name when it is needed, and caring for members of God's family (see chapter 8), we are seen for our good works and God is glorified (Matthew 5:16).

The ministry of helps is service—where, when, to whomever, for however long, whatever the need. This is where the new-born (spiritual and physical) begins to function. And as the believer matures in the Lord, in obedience to the Word of God, the Holy Spirit may call him into a leadership role in this function of helps, or into another function.

The Holy Spirit's call has sometimes come from an audible voice, but more often from the inward witness of the Spirit's agreement with the individual desire, prompted by one's personal gift. This is yet another confirmation of the fact that a person can best manifest God's love through the individual gracious gift of joy (personal gift) that God has given him.

Once a person is aware of the Holy Spirit's call to function in a leadership role, helps or another, *the Holy Spirit will also tell other mature believers* of this call. Then, when the proper time comes (be it a week, a month, or many years hence), these mature believers will "set him apart" for this new service.

An outstanding scriptural example of the above is to be found in Acts 13:1-5. While the Body was assembled (v. 1) and worshiping the Lord and fasting (v. 2), "the Holy Spirit said, Separate now for Me Barnabas and Saul for the work *to which I have called them.*"

The prerequisites are clear: *the men had previously been called by the Lord.* Now they were being recognized or acknowledged as *having been set in a particular function by the Body* itself.

Those who would set themselves in a function without being recognized or set apart by other godly men need to be reminded of Jesus' parable of the ambitious guest who took the high place before he was bidden. The parable is found in Luke 14, and verse 11 states, "For everyone who tries to honor himself shall be humbled; and he who humbles himself shall be honored" *(The Living Bible).*

It is important not to confuse the ten *functions* with the seven *personal gifts* we have been discussing in the earlier chapters. They are not the same, though some are similar in name. For instance, there is the *personal gift of teaching;* there is also the *function of teacher.* There is the *personal gift of ruling/administration;* there is also the *function of governments.* There is the *personal gift of prophecy;* there is also the *function of prophet.*

The basic difference between the two is this: the personal gift is a gift given to an individual; whereas the ministry gift (function) is a gift given to the Body of believers as a whole. So you see, *one is a personal gift and one is a corporate gift.*

For example, a person who possesses the personal gift of administration may be called of the Holy Spirit into the function of administration. When this happens, the call is always confirmed by other godly men. Dr. Ted Engstrom, as we have previously mentioned, possesses the personal gift of administration. The Holy Spirit called or impressed upon him that he should be serving in an administrative capacity. This was confirmed many years ago when the godly men who made up the board of Youth For Christ asked him to become their chief administrator. This was again confirmed recently when the World Vision board of directors asked Dr. Engstrom to serve as their chief administrator, the president of the organization.

However, the Holy Spirit may call a person who possesses the personal gift of administration into a different function. I also possess the personal gift of administration, but am serving in a leadership function in helps. As a mother, I served in helps while I was raising my children. I *opened my home to share* with others the blessings I had received. I drove kids to choir practice, played the piano for Sunday school, typed the church bulletin, took my children to visit nursing homes, etc. Then one day God spoke to me and I began to write. First I wrote short magazine articles, which men of God in the publishing field printed in Christian magazines. Two years ago other men of God accepted my first book for publication, and now this second one. By so doing they recognized and confirmed my call to function in the leadership role of helps.

A local radio personality, Dr. Vernon, who possesses the *personal gift of teaching,* has been called of the Holy Spirit, and set apart by godly men unto the *function of teacher.* Then there is Dr. Blizzard, one of the prominent non-Jewish Hebrew educators of this decade, whose *personal gift is prophecy.* He has been called by the Holy Spirit and set apart by godly men to serve in the *function of teacher* via seminars and television across the nation.

Notice the *seeming* incongruity. In the first illustration, Dr. Engstrom and I both possess the *same personal gift,* but are operating in *different functions*—he in governments and me in helps. The following chart illustrates how this principle works:

CHART TWO

Persons with the *personal gift* of . . .	*approach* everything they do in this manner . . .	no matter which *function* they have been called to:
Ruling/ administration (Dr. Engstrom) (Myself)	He is well organized about his person, his possessions, his area of responsibility. He is goal-oriented, inclined toward short-range, intermediate-range, and long-range goals and check points. He is efficient in his use of delegation.	*Evangelists* *Pastors* *Apostles* *Prophets* *Teachers* *Miracles* *Gifts of healings* *Helps* (Myself) *Governments* (Engstrom) *Diversities of tongues*

Now for the second part of this seeming incongruity. Here Dr. Vernon and Dr. Blizzard, who possess *different personal gifts* are serving in the *same function of teacher.* This will be true in every function, i.e., there will be men and women called to any one of the functions who possess a variety of personal gifts.

In this regard, I have known pastors who possessed the personal gift of exhorting, whose ministry was characterized by an emphasis upon counsel and encouragement. I also knew a pastor whose personal gift was ministry. In serving his people, he spawned a variety of programs that offered practical assistance to each member of the church family. When my husband, Bob (whose personal gift is mercy), served in the function of pastor, he projected special concern for the hurts and needs of his congregation as well as for people around the world. My son, Terry, whose personal gift is teaching, has also been called and set apart in the function of pastor. It's a joy to me to hear him speak, for his ministry is characterized by well-thought-through and well-presented Bible studies.

The following chart provides a clearly defined outline of the manner in which persons with each of the seven personal gifts would approach the function of pastor (or function of teacher, as in the illustration of Dr. Vernon and Dr. Blizzard).

Just as parents with differing personal gifts will "parent" in different ways, so will persons called to one of the ten functions (listed at the first of this chapter) operate differently. This brings to the Body a variety of emphases that complement one another.

Let me give another example. The person with the personal gift of mercy who is functioning as an evangelist will spread the Good News in an entirely different way from that of the evangelist with the personal gift of prophecy. This is necessary, because there are many unbelievers who would not respond to the "mercy-approach" evangelist, who will respond to the "prophecy-approach" evangelist, and vice versa.

All of this is as God in his wisdom foresaw. That is why he calls

THERE IS A FUNCTION FOR EVERYONE

CHART THREE

Would tend to emphasize powerful sermons exposing sin, with warnings of judgment, and proclaiming right living.

PROPHECY

Would tend to emphasize programs to give practical assistance to each member of the church.

MINISTRY

Would tend to emphasize in-depth Bible studies, stressing the importance of clearly defined words.

TEACHING

Would tend to emphasize methods of encouragement in order to help each member apply scriptural principles to his daily life.

EXHORTING

PASTOR

Would tend to emphasize generous programs of financial assistance to the needy, to missionaries, and to other ministries.

GIVING

ADMINISTRATION

Would tend to emphasize goal-oriented organization with efficiently delegated departments.

MERCY

Would tend to emphasize special outreaches which would identify and bring comfort to the hurting.

a person to fill a function who possesses the personal gift that will best meet the needs at that particular time.

In fact, a good illustration of this was mentioned in the first chapter. Dr. Bob Pierce, the founder and first administrator of World Vision, with his personal gift of mercy, was the ideal man to found such an organization. Dr. Bob has since died, leaving behind an outstanding heritage: an organization that is presently caring for nearly half a million orphans.

Can you see how God needed a man with the personal gift of mercy as the chief administrator of this caring-for-people organization in those early days? And now, today, with its caring ministries in nearly 100 countries, and its over 700 employees in this country alone, God has called Dr. Engstrom, a man with the personal gift of administration, to be the organization's chief administrator.

I think you are now beginning to see how important it is for us to understand how each of the numerous combinations of personal gifts and functions is needed to *fully* equip the Body of Christ. That is why it is important—as I have already cautioned—that we not confuse a function in the Body of Christ with our own personal gift.

If you carefully follow the suggestions for studying the "Style Guides" at the conclusion of each of chapters 2 through 8, you will be able to *know* your personal gift. When you have done this, you are ready to begin serving the Body in the function of helps by giving assistance in any way you can.

You should serve in that function "joyfully" until the Lord's return or until the Holy Spirit calls you into a leadership role, either in helps or in one of the other nine functions.

So serve the Lord with a joyous gladness—where you are! He always rewards faithfulness.

TWELVE

JOY, SERVICE, POWER FOR PARENT AND CHILD

Charlene laid down the pages of this chapter, her face aglow. "I get it!" she said, "I understand. For the very first time I understand!"

I turned from my typewriter. "OK, tell me."

She beamed with excitement. "My personal gift . . . when I know what it is, it enables me to approach every situation with joy. Great joy! Right?"

"Right," I said. "Go on."

"And when I serve God in my function, in the place he wants me to be, I can do it effectively. . . right again?"

"Right again."

Her words tumbled out. "And when I operate from my personal gift . . . and I'm functioning where he wants me to be . . ." she paused for breath, "then there'll be power in my life. Right?"

"But you left out something."

She looked disappointed. "What's that?"

"Charlene, you must be living in the Word of God. You must be reading the Word *and* obeying it. And *then*—just like you said, you'll have joy . . . service . . . and power."

Charlene smiled happily. "I know. I know. And for the first time in my life I'm beginning to see it happen."

Charlene understood what I am sharing with you: the definitions of your personal gift, your function, and the connection between these and the manifested power of the Holy Spirit. But just in case you may still have some unanswered questions, this chapter outlines the above concept into six sections, each one based on a clarifying principle.

PRINCIPLE NUMBER ONE

The KEY to your personal gift is JOY. So if what you are doing is not being done in joy, you are not properly utilizing your personal gift.

This principle is inviolable, because when you are effectively operating from your personal gift, God will infuse you with joy and thus strength. He promises that you can "run and not be weary; and . . . walk, and not faint" (Isaiah 40:31). Operating according to the positive aspects of this principle will result in minimal weariness and maximum effectiveness in all that you do.

The reverse is also true. If you try to imitate someone else's personal gift, or attempt to move into a function to which the Holy Spirit has not called you, or choose a profession which does not lend itself to your approach (your personal gift), you are likely to become weary with your "well doing." If this happens you will experience neither total effectiveness nor exuberant joy.

Let me give an illustration of this as it occurred in a professional role.

An expanding organization with a large secretarial pool engaged me to become editor for their magazine. I had no sooner assumed my position when I became aware of the dissension and strife among the secretaries. They were outspoken in their criticisms of Carla, the office manager. At first I didn't understand why, for I found her to be pleasant and helpful. Carla was herself an excellent secretary and receptionist, but she was clearly experiencing difficulties in managing the office.

"Carla doesn't distribute the work evenly," I heard one girl tell another. "Besides, she spends too much time going over yesterday's work."

"I noticed," the other secretary answered. "And she's always taking work home. I don't understand how, when some of the girls have practically nothing to do. . . ."

It was a relief to all when Carla was reassigned and became the personal secretary to the executive director and Lila was hired as our new office manager. Within days there was a different atmosphere in the office.

Lila quickly assumed responsibility for the running of the entire office. She appointed teams for the various tasks. She delegated practically everything, making good use of all the resources available. Within a few weeks unity was restored and goals were being reached in record time. And even though Lila did very little of the actual work herself, she was admired and respected by the entire office force.

What brought about the difference? Though both Carla and Lila had operated in the same position, with the same staff, only Lila was able to do so with joy. Carla, possessing the personal gift of ministry, was not comfortable delegating work to others and soon found herself snowed under with the excessive "showing" and "doing" of tasks that could have been done by others.

On the other hand, Lila had the personal gift of administration. And the needs of the position, which had become burdensome for Carla, merely served as challenges to Lila. The result was that Lila, who simply utilized her personal gift, was filled with joy by fulfilling the duties of the position.

PRINCIPLE NUMBER TWO

The function into which the Holy Spirit calls you will always be a place where you will effectively and joyfully activate your personal gift.

The Holy Spirit does not operate at cross purposes with himself. He has provided you with your personal gift. He has called you to a function. Therefore, the logical and "theological" (if you want to call it that) result is that you will be properly fitted and slotted to function for him in the place he has planned. You will be able to do so effectively, and with joy.

Harold Stowe is a good demonstration of this principle. His personal gift was mercy, and when he heard the call go out from his local church for "short-term" missionaries, he responded. As a contractor for low-income housing, Mr. Stowe found himself eagerly anticipating what became his annual volunteering for overseas service. For many years he functioned in helps as he raised his family and assisted the poor in their housing needs.

Then the Holy Spirit spoke to Harold Stowe. Harold told his wife, "I am finding my work on the islands much more satisfying than here in the States."

She smiled. "I can tell. You are always so happy when it's time to go again . . . and you're increasingly reluctant about coming back."

Harold took a deep breath. "I really believe God is calling me to go to the islands to live."

The following year when the Missions Conference was selecting personnel to send to the field, the committee chairman approached Mr. Stowe. "After much prayer," he began, "we believe God wants us to send you to the South Pacific to assist our full-time missionaries. We believe he wants you to give leadership to the building of churches, orphanages, and schools on several islands. . . ."

Harold smiled. "Just like in chapter 13 of the book of Acts," he said. "I will go with great joy, because God has already shown me that is what he wants me to do."

PRINCIPLE NUMBER THREE

When you exercise your PERSONAL GIFT (Romans 12:6-8) through the FUNCTION/MINISTRY into which the Holy Spirit calls you (Ephesians 4:11; 1 Corinthians 12:28, 29), then the Holy Spirit determines which MANIFESTATIONS (1 Corinthians 12:8-10) are to most advantageously *flow through you to the receiver.*

It may be that we have assumed a responsibility in a function to which we have not been called, or have become involved in activities which detract from our ability to concentrate on our personal gift. We are instructed in Romans 12 to concentrate on whatever our gift is.

When we do so the Holy Spirit can then call us into a place where we may function with the fullness of joy, and thus in the strength and power of the Lord. So when (as per Principle Number Three) a person knows and operates from his personal gift in the function to which the Holy Spirit calls him, then the Holy Spirit will effectively flow through him.

Let's read 1 Corinthians 12:1, 4-6 from the Weymouth Version: "Now about spiritual gifts, brethren, I would not have you ignorant" (v. 1). In Weymouth, as in many of our English translations, the Greek word *pneumatikon* is rendered, "spiritual gifts." However, the word "gifts" does not appear in the Greek. It was placed in our English versions by the translators. In some of the newer translations a more accurate rendering is given of both the word and the phrase: "Now concerning *[pneumatikon]* things pertaining to the Holy Spirit. . . ."

Chart #4 gives verses 4, 5, and 6.

CHART FOUR

Seven Personal Gifts	Ten Functions	Nine Manifestations
"Now there are various kinds of gifts *[charismata]*" (v. 4).	". . . various kinds of official service *[diakonion]*" (v. 5).	". . . various kinds of effects *[energema]*" (v. 6).
Gracious gift of joy given to each believer, through which we approach every situation (Rom. 12:6-8).	Function or office into which the Holy Spirit calls each child of God who is being led by him (1 Cor. 12:26-28; Eph. 4:11).	Results produced by the Holy Spirit through each child of God who is operating by his personal gift in the proper function (1 Cor. 12:7-10).

This is not to say that the only time the Holy Spirit will manifest himself through a person is when he is operating by his personal gift in the function to which he has been called; but I do believe that the Holy Spirit most frequently manifests himself through those who are operating in their personal gifts and who are serving in the function the Holy Spirit has called them to, *and* who have been taught to *expect* the Holy Spirit to manifest himself. Then as the person walks in obedience to the Word of God, he is a prepared vessel through which the Holy Spirit can manifest himself in the way he determines that will best meet the needs.

An excellent illustration of this truth comes to mind from an incident told me by a missionary. He and his wife and young child were new arrivals at a mission station in the heart of South America. They knew little about the culture or customs of the aboriginal tribe to which they had been sent to minister, and nothing at all of the language or dialect.

The missionary was a godly man and had taught his young boy to expect God to manifest himself supernaturally when a need presented itself. He was, himself, an inspirational model to his son.

Shortly after their arrival in the village, the child became attracted to the sickly old chief who could no longer be up and about and who was confined to his hut. The chief and his family were resistant to all efforts of the missionaries to share the gospel with them. But the little boy continued to go daily to the old chief's hut and sing to him. Though neither understood the other, a warm relationship sprang up.

Concerning this, the boy said to his father, "God sent us here to win the chief and his people to Jesus . . . didn't he?"

"That's right, Norris, he did."

"Then I'll keep singing to him about Jesus."

So for several days Norris sang, "Jesus loves me . . ." to the impassive old chieftain.

Then one day something happened that broke through the

man's shell of resistance. Norris was singing in English, when quite suddenly he heard himself singing words that were strange to him. Though he didn't know the language, it sounded like the language he had heard the people around him speak.

He liked the sounds he was making, so he kept singing the words over and over to the tune of his beloved song. As he sang, the boy was startled to see tears trickling down the old chief's face. Soon the chief motioned to the young man who served as interpreter for the missionary.

"Tell me what it means . . ." the chief said, quoting the words of the song exactly as the boy had been singing them.

When he heard that the boy was singing of Jesus' love for him, his old heart broke and he received Jesus into his life. With the chief's conversion, the tribe also confessed Jesus as Lord.

This is a marvelous example of a child with the personal gift of mercy who was operating in the function of helps. And as he faithfully obeyed the Holy Spirit's moving, he was given words to sing that he had not learned, in a language he did not know, that resulted in the salvation of the old chief.

The child actually expected the old chief to receive Jesus, though he did not anticipate how it would happen. The Holy Spirit took the boy's faithfulness and expectations and added the supernatural, which resulted in the miracle of new birth to the old man and his tribe.

Chart #5 on page 146 illustrates this.

PRINCIPLE NUMBER FOUR

The manifestation of the Holy Spirit operates only as the Holy Spirit wills. I cannot control this movement or operation of the Holy Spirit.

Only the Holy Spirit knows when, where, and how he can most effectively move to glorify the Father. But it is certain that *he does know* when, where, and how and to whom he should manifest himself. He will manifest himself through anyone he chooses, any way he chooses.

SEVEN STYLES OF PARENTING

CHART FIVE

Personal Gifts (Romans 12:6-8)	*Functions* (Ephesians 4:11; 1 Corinthians 12:28)	Ways the Holy Spirit *manifests* himself (1 Corinthians 12:8-10)
Prophecy *Ministry* *Teaching* *Exhorting* *Giving* *Ruling/ Administration* *Mercy* (Norris, with his personal gift of *mercy,* is functioning in *helps.* The Holy Spirit then manifests himself in whatever way will best meet the need and bring glory to our Father in heaven. In the illustration given [of Norris and the tribal chief], the Holy Spirit chose to manifest himself through a tongue unknown to Norris.)	*Evangelists:* Declaring the good news of salvation *Pastors:* Shepherding a congregation *Apostles:* Establishing new congregations *Prophets:* Revealing the messages of God *Teachers:* Instructing through didactic discourses *Miracles:* Demonstrating supernatural deeds of the Holy Spirit *Gifts of healings:* Administrating physical/emotional healing *Helps:* Rendering assistance *Governments:* Coordinating/ integrating the affairs of the church *Diversities of tongues:* Speaking and/or interpreting other languages	● *Word of wisdom* Revelation of God's Word/purpose/plan ● *Word of knowledge* Divine insight of unlearned knowledge ● *Faith* Acting in obedience beyond one's natural understanding ● *Gifts of healing* Administrating God's healing power ● *Working of miracles* Laws of nature are altered, suspended, or controlled ● *Prophecy* Speaking to edify, exhort, or comfort ● *Discerning of spirits* Recognizing activities in the spirit realm ● *Kinds of tongues* Utterance in languages (of men or of angels, 1 Cor. 13:1) unknown to the speaker ● *Interpretation of tongues* Interpretation of unknown languages

JOY, SERVICE, POWER FOR PARENT AND CHILD

Some years ago my mother was diagnosed as having a brain tumor. After the diagnosis had been confirmed by X-ray, she was sent home to rest until time for surgery, which was scheduled in Chicago. The tumor had so unsettled her equilibrium that she was unable to walk or even stand without assistance.

One afternoon my mother's pastor, a very conservative man, along with four of his elders, came to visit her at home. The elders prayed, "Father, if it be thy will, heal Mrs. Andrews. . . ."

However, the pastor prayed, "Father, Mrs. Andrews is your child and I thank you and praise you for what you are going to do in her body. . . ."

My mother was startled by the pointedness, the confidence of the pastor's prayer, but said nothing. Since the surgery date was two weeks away, my father took my mother to Arkansas for a week of vacation before going on to Chicago for their appointment. They were thinking, "This may be the last time we can do something like this together."

Since my mother was rather weak and unstable, as well as quite nauseated, my father had to practically carry her out to the car. Enroute, when they stopped at a service station, Mother had to be helped into and out of the restroom. Back in the car she went to sleep and my father drove on for several hours before he stopped.

"Would you like to eat something?" he asked.

My mother awoke and looked around. "Yes, I would. I'm quite hungry." By the time he had gotten out of the car and had come around to her side, she had opened the door and was climbing out. He looked at her in amazement as she walked into the restaurant, ate a hearty meal, and went back to the car.

They drove on to Arkansas and had a wonderful week, then went on to Chicago. After the surgeon had taken X-rays, he brought my mother and father into his office.

He held up two X-rays. "Mr. and Mrs. Andrews," he began, "this picture was taken in Kalamazoo. Notice the dark mass— that's the tumor. Very distinct. Now look at this picture. No mass. Only an area that looks empty, like an air pocket *where the tumor was*. But it's not there anymore. It's gone!"

Back home the pastor, Brother Langdon, told my mother, "The Lord told me that if I would come and pray for you that *he would heal you*. One other time in my ministry, when I was a missionary in Africa, a healing like that was manifested when God sent me to pray."

The Holy Spirit himself had chosen the man through whom his healing power would flow. The Holy Spirit chose the time. He also chose the one who was to be the recipient of his healing flow. The pastor had nothing to do with the transaction as far as making the choice of how or when the Holy Spirit would manifest himself. All he had to do was be obedient and speak the words God told him to pray.

Brother Langdon, who was serving in the *function of pastor, not in the function of gifts of healings,* was used by the Holy Spirit as a vessel to administer the gifts of healing to my mother.

Chart #6 illustrates this:

CHART SIX

Functions	Ways the Holy Spirit *manifests* himself
Evangelists	Word of wisdom
Pastors	Word of knowledge
Apostles	Faith
Prophets	Gifts of healing
Teachers	Working of miracles
Miracles	Prophecy
Gifts of healings	Discerning of spirits
Helps	Kinds of tongues
Governments	Interpretations of tongues
Diversities of tongues	

Langdon •

*Manifestation of the Holy Spirit in the previous illustration.

On the other hand, Oral Roberts has often told of how God called him to serve in the function of gifts of healings. Consequently, Brother Roberts has frequently been used as a vessel through which the Holy Spirit has manifested himself to others in gifts of healing. However, even though a man is called to function in one of the ten functions that is *similar in name* to one of the nine manifestations, this does not limit the Holy Spirit. He will always manifest himself through any person he chooses, in the way that will most benefit the recipient, whether it be gifts of healing, discerning of spirits, word of wisdom, or any of the six others.

For instance, Harold Stowe, whom I have previously mentioned, was once just beginning to put a roof on a new orphanage when a tropical hurricane approached. At the moving of the Holy Spirit, Harold spoke to that storm in the name of Jesus and it split and went around the orphanage on both sides, leaving the orphanage untouched and dry.

Chart #7 illustrates this example:

CHART SEVEN

	Functions	Ways the Holy Spirit *manifests* himself
	Evangelists	• Word of wisdom
	Pastors	• Word of knowledge
	Apostles	
	Prophets	• Faith
Stowe •	Teachers	• Gifts of healing
	Miracles	• Working of miracles
*Manifestation of the Holy Spirit in the previous illustration.	Gifts of healings	• Prophecy
	• Helps •	• Discerning of spirits
	Governments	
	Diversities of tongues	• Kinds of tongues
		• Interpretations of tongues

In both of the previous illustrations, we saw people who were sensitive to the leadership of the Holy Spirit, which is the mark of Christian maturity. As the child of God spends time getting to know the Holy Spirit, yielding himself to and allowing himself to be led and guided by him, the Holy Spirit will supernaturally manifest himself in power. And it will be through the obedient vessels that the power of the Holy Spirit will flow unhindered.

Sometimes these manifestations will be of a spectacular nature, as in the incident above. Sometimes they will not *seem* to be of such dimensions. Such was the case last week when Bob was deep in his studying, in preparation for teaching Bible study the following day, while David was working in the yard.

David was ready to use the lawnmower, but when he tried to start it, his efforts were in vain. He entered Bob's office and said, "The lawnmower won't start. What shall I do?"

Without a moment's hesitation, Bob spoke in words that were prompted by the Holy Spirit. "I'll get the hairdryer and dry it out."

David protested. "But it's not wet. It's been in the garage since I last used it."

Bob said nothing more, but got the hairdryer. He focused the stream of air on the carburetor and coils for a couple of minutes. "Now try it," he said.

With a single pull on the starter, the lawnmower roared into life. Afterward, Bob said to me, "I didn't even have time to think of what might be wrong with the mower before this word about the hairdryer moved strongly into my mind. I believe the Holy Spirit gave me a word of knowledge for that particular moment because I needed to use my time right then for preparation to teach the Bible study group."

PRINCIPLE NUMBER FIVE

As you are moving in your personal gift, don't strive or be anxious about where you should be serving in the Body. Serve joyfully in helps until the Holy Spirit directs you into either a leadership role in helps or in another function.

When the Holy Spirit chooses to call you into either a leadership function in helps or into another function, *you will know*. At this point, you must remain yielded and patient. Utilize the precious months and years you have to assist your children by leading them in helps. (See chapter 8.) Model for them a godly parent who is willing to serve any place at any time, whenever the Lord speaks.

As you do remain joyfully patient and faithful in your service, in due time the Holy Spirit will speak to other godly people about your service, and they will call you into a leadership role. By having been patient and faithful during those months or years, you will then be ready for other opportunities when they come.

The Apostle Paul himself is our example of this principle. When the Lord called him to himself, while he was in Damascus, Paul knew that he was to bear Jesus' "name before the Gentiles, and kings, and the children of Israel" (Acts 9:15).

But the elapsed time between God's call until Paul was set apart by other godly men was between ten and fifteen years. Paul must have been faithful in preparing himself during those years, for when God spoke to him through Barnabas, he was ready.

A personal illustration regarding the fact that these callings are in God's timing, not ours, may be helpful. As I have told you, I functioned in helps for many years, until such time as the Holy Spirit called me into a leadership role in helps and confirmed that call by godly men. As I was faithful in that regard, about two years ago God spoke to me and told me that he was calling me to the function of teacher.

This excited me, and I immediately began making what turned out to be abortive efforts to hasten God's process. But all my efforts to "help" God move his schedule along came to naught. I soon realized what I was doing, and began to prepare myself while waiting for God's timing. I am still doing that, realizing that as I continue to make and keep myself ready (be it one year or ten) then he will speak to other godly people who will then set me apart for his work in this new function.

PRINCIPLE NUMBER SIX

Once a person is called into a specific leadership function, he *may not* remain there the rest of his life. God may call him into a different leadership function.

The Holy Spirit is not capricious. He is consistent and logical. He also sees the entire Body, while we see only a portion, "a hand or an eye," to use the apostle's analogy. So when the Holy Spirit determines that one faithful person can now more effectively minister to the Body in another function, the Spirit will once again speak to him.

So you see, the process then repeats itself. The person is called by the Holy Spirit to another function. Then, in time (be it weeks or years), godly men confirm the call.

For example: My husband Bob was called to function for a number of years as a pastor. But the time came when Bob was called to move into the leadership role of helps and he became an editor for the David C. Cook Publishing Company. Bob is a very skilled and creative editor and writer. In the editorial position where he was placed, the Holy Spirit had work for him to do.

Although today Bob teaches a regular Bible study and is called upon to preach from time to time, he is still functioning as a leader in helps. He continues to assist others in the Body by helping them write and publish their stories and dreams.

It is important to note that just because you do some teaching doesn't mean you've been called to the function of teacher. Or just because you do some administrating doesn't mean you've been called to the function of governments. For example, Bob is a writer, but last weekend when the dishwasher stopped working, he did some plumbing and repaired it. But that did not make him a plumber.

By knowing what our personal gift is, and operating in the function to which we have been called, we become free. That is, we are freed and enabled to be ourselves. We will neither strive to be like others, nor envy their accomplishments. Instead, we will rejoice with them in the unity that results as each of us allows our gifts to blend into that oneness of the Body for which Jesus prayed in John 17.

However, if I am not using my personal gift, nor functioning where the Holy Spirit has called me—either because of ignorance or resistance—the Body of Christ will be weakened and become imbalanced. The Apostle Paul speaks of the necessity of this unity in Ephesians 4:16: "From whom the whole body fitly joined together and compacted by that which every joint supplieth, according to the effectual working in the measure of *every part.*" This clearly means our parts are needed. Both yours and mine.

For it is only when we, as individual members of the Body, understand our personal gifts and functions and share this knowledge with others that the Body of Christ can come together. But when this does happen, there will be an unprecedented coordination and dynamic that will edify and unify the totality of the Body of Christ.

In the light of all that precedes, I can only speak to you what God has spoken to me: be faithful. Abide in the Word of God (as Jesus commanded in John 15). Open yourself up to the Holy Spirit, yielding yourself to his every urging and leading. Don't attempt to copy others. Mind only what the Holy Spirit says and "magnify" the function he has given you.

The Living Bible says this very clearly: "I advise you to obey only the Holy Spirit's instructions. He will tell you where to go and what to do, and then you won't always be doing the wrong things" (Galatians 5:16).

THIRTEEN

SHOWING YOUR CHILD HOW TO SERVE

Everything was in readiness. It was time for the service to begin. The side door opened and the tiny pianist clippity-clopped across the room in her twice-too-large high heels, while trying to keep her overly large skirt from dragging on the floor. She reached the piano bench and clambered on top, heaved a long sigh, and poised her hands on the keyboard.

The choir director struggled to straighten his tie, which was lumpily tied on the white shirt that nearly reached the floor. The single choir member pulled her cat to an upright position on the seat beside her. And all the while the preacher impatiently paced back and forth on the "platform," occasionally thumping the huge Bible he had set before him on his cardboard "podium."

Lined up before the preacher's

prophetic visage were several rows of "pews" consisting of two benches, three straight chairs, and five small, different styles of rocking chairs. A conglomerate "congregation" of assorted dolls and stuffed animals was seated attentively in most of them.

In the front row, seated by himself, was one dark-haired little boy. Peeking at this "church scene" from the hallway, I heard the little boy ask, "Why can't I ever be anybody?"

The "Reverend" Terry stopped his pacing and fixed the "parishioner" with a stony gaze. "Because you don't know enough." Then he resumed his ministerial pacing.

Keith, the choir director, added, "When you learn our songs then you can sing with us."

Alice agreed with a knowing nod. "And then you can sit in my kitty's seat."

Trish didn't pause at the keyboard, but spoke over her shoulder to the hopeful volunteer. "Someday I'll get another piano, or maybe an organ. Then you can play one of them. . . ."

"But I want to be somebody, *now!*" David muttered in weary frustration.

Have you ever felt that way? That you wanted to be somebody, anybody, in the kingdom of God? Well, I have. But for many years I thought you had to be something "extraordinary" to be "special" in God's kingdom. And, since I thought I didn't qualify, I felt like David: frustrated, with no place to "be a part of" whatever it was that God was doing.

Then one day I made the discovery that God likens his kingdom to our physical bodies.

God tells us in his Word:

> Our bodies have many parts, but the many parts make up only one body when they are all put together. So it is with the "body" of Christ. Each of us is a part of the one body of Christ. . . . Yes, the body has many parts, not just one part. If the foot says, "I am not a part of the body because I am not a hand," that does not make it any less a part of the body. And what would you think if you heard an ear say, "I am not part of the body because I am only an ear, and not an eye"? Would that make it any less a part of the body? Suppose the whole body were an eye—then how

would you hear? Or if your whole body were just one big ear, how could you smell anything?

But that isn't the way God has made us. He has made many parts for our bodies and has put each part just where he wants it. What a strange thing a body would be if it had only one part! So he has made many parts, but still there is only one body.

The eye can never say to the hand, "I don't need you." The head can't say to the feet, "I don't need you."

And some of the parts that seem weakest and least important are really the most necessary. Yes, we are especially glad to have some parts that seem rather odd! And we carefully protect from the eyes of others those parts that should not be seen, while of course the parts that may be seen do not require this special care. So God has put the body together in such a way that extra honor and care are given to those parts that might otherwise seem less important. This makes for happiness among the parts, so that the parts have the same care for each other that they do for themselves. If one part suffers, all parts suffer with it, and if one part is honored, all the parts are glad.

Now here is what I am trying to say: All of you together are the one body of Christ and each one of you is a separate and necessary part of it (1 Corinthians 12:12-27, *The Living Bible*).

Members and organs of a physical body don't have to "wait" until they know more, sing better, or until they are furnished with additional equipment before they can become important parts of the body. Not at all. Each part of the physical body is as vital to its overall well-being at conception as it is when it attains full adulthood.

This is as true with the Body of Christ as it is with our physical bodies.

As was mentioned in the last chapter, each member of the Body of Christ receives a function as soon as he becomes a member of the Body. That initial function is helps. Some would have it that the function of helps is the least important in the Body. This position does not coincide with the Scripture passage we just read. For there it said, "the parts that seem the least important are really the most necessary."

And helps is a part that is necessary to the smooth-running operation of every other function in Christ's Body.

The definition of the word itself gives credence to this stance. According to Webster, the word "help" means: "to make easier (for a person) to do something; to ease or share the labor of; to make it easier (for something) to exist, happen, develop, improve, etc." Specifically, "(a) to make more effective, larger, etc.; aid the growth of; promote. (b) To cause improvement in; to be responsible for; to serve."

Could it be that the function of helps has sometimes been demeaned or scorned because it was little understood, or even misunderstood? I think this is undoubtedly the case. And yet, the Body of Christ is replete with all sorts of illustrations and examples that point out both the place and importance of helps.

Almost every imaginable profession possesses its share of those who are operating in the Body of Christ in the function of helps—from the medical profession to manufacturing; from the home to the White House staff; and every walk of life in between has its share of those who serve in this important function. Let me delineate a few, some in the public eye, others not; some in the leadership role of helps, others not; some salaried, others not—but each one making the Body of Christ more effective by his or her faithfulness in the function of helps. For example:

Judge Davis is a publicly recognized figure who projects a Christian witness in government. He is responsible for interpreting and enforcing the laws of our land, thus making it possible for you and me to live "a quiet and peaceable life in all godliness and honesty."

My husband's friend, Guy Mayo, is an entrepreneur who successfully buys, develops, and sells large tracts of land. He helps the Body of Christ by giving hundreds of thousands of dollars annually to Christian organizations.

Jackie Mitchum is the Guest Hostess for the Christian Broadcast Network's "700 Club." Jackie schedules guests for the program who will bring glory to God, and who will help the TV viewers to live and project a more dynamic witness.

Kathleen Marvin is a wife, mother, and homemaker. In addition to the helpful, loving care she provides for her husband and son, she helps the Body by initiating quality music programs for her church, which enrich and edify the worshipers.

As you begin to see the importance and scope of the function of helps, you can realize the necessity for as many of us as possible to be involved in this function that ministers within and to the Body of Christ, because the categories don't stop with the people and professions I have named. You yourself can think of and name a dozen or so others who function in helps. There are janitors and custodians. Which reminds me of Leroy, whose personal gift is administration. . . .

Leroy had been retired for several years when he approached the senior pastor one day with this unusual request: "I would like the privilege of caring for the buildings and grounds of our church complex," he said.

The pastor looked at the little man before him. "The privilege, you say? What do you mean, Leroy?"

Leroy waved his hand, indicating the four- or five-acre grounds. "This is God's property," he said. "I'd like to make it into a garden spot. I'd like to make the interior woodwork shine. . . . I'd like our church to be a place where God would be pleased to dwell."

Needless to say, Leroy was afforded the opportunity. He enlisted a number of volunteers, and together they fulfilled his goal. Never before had the church complex been more lovely and attractive. Leroy was serving the Body of Christ in the function of helps.

Then there are those dedicated people who produce the thousands of Bible and teaching cassettes and tapes that go around the world to further extend the ministry of Christ. These people function in helps. Markus is one of these remarkable people who serves us all so well. He joyfully gives of his time in the "Tape Room" to "do his part. . . ." Almost any time of the day when you might happen past the Tape Room you will hear his cheerful voice lifted in song, or his whistled rendition of, "The Joy of the Lord Is My Strength."

Sylvia is a widow whose personal gift is exhorting. She writes letters—to the sick, the hurting, and shut-ins. She assists the staff of a Christian radio ministry. Through her thoughtfully written letters of encouragement, she ministers the love of God to the hundreds she writes to each month.

There isn't space to list or enumerate all those who function in helps. Why don't you pause for a moment and name a few whom you know personally. I'll give you a few more to get you started: telephone counselors for Christian radio and television programs, choir members, ushers, nursery workers, visitation people, church bus drivers, nursing home attendants, foster parents, lawyers, church pianists, organists, church musicians, and others.

And most certainly, the warm-hearted people who are always inviting folks into their homes for a warm meal and fellowship. My husband tells of the time when he was in Australia for a couple of weeks. He was an officer in the U. S. Merchant Marines, and didn't know anybody in Sydney, Australia.

He went to a large church in the city, and after the service a sweet Christian couple invited him into their home. They fed him and invited him back. Their home was so "homelike" that he returned several more times during his stay in the city and spent the afternoons fellowshiping with them. Certainly that couple who "made it easier" for a sailor a long way from home was operating in the function of helps.

"But these illustrations are all about adults," you might remind me. "What about children? How do my children function in helps?" The answer to the question is, "First they need a model."

Before children can effectively function in helps, they need an example to follow. Let me introduce you to the Wayne Reed family and show you what I mean.

Wayne Reed possesses the personal gift of administration and functions in a leadership role in helps. For the past dozen years he has served as head usher for his church. This is no small task, for he leads a well-trained corps of twenty ushers.

Wayne's wife, Priscilla Reed, possesses the personal gift of giving. She functions in helps by baking whole wheat breads and other health foods and selling them to the local market. And what does she do with the money she thus makes? She purchases new clothing and gives it to the church's "Good Samaritan Shop" to be handed out to those in need.

Sixteen-year-old Albert's personal gift is prophecy. He functions in helps by assisting his father in his ushering role. Vickie, fourteen, has the personal gift of ministry. She serves in helps by doing all of her mother's housekeeping chores on the days her mother bakes.

Twelve-year-old Corrie, whose personal gift is mercy, functions in helps by baby-sitting for the children of the pastoral staff whenever they need her. The entire Reed family happily functions in helps in different areas, each with a different personal gift. This is as it should be, because "All of you together are the one body of Christ and each one of you is a separate and necessary part of it" (1 Corinthians 12:27, TLB).

Do you have children old enough to mow the lawn? Have them mow the neighbor's lawn sometime, for no particular reason other than, "Jesus loves you," they can tell that neighbor, "and so do I." We have a beautiful Muslim family living next door. Occasionally our son mows their lawn for no other reason than the above.

Who mows your pastor's lawn? Does your son need a model to get him started functioning in helps? Then go with him. Help him mow and trim the pastor's lawn. Then plant some flowers in his yard. Everyone will benefit and God will be glorified.

I know of a small boy who lived on a farm a few miles out in the country. The family was homesteading the land and they were not as yet financially stable. The mother wanted to give something to a mission school in Bolivia, but had little to give. She mentioned this to her husband one day.

He said, "You've got several chickens. Why don't you gather the eggs and sell them, then give your egg money to the Lord?"

The boy overheard the conversation. "And I'll go out and gather the eggs," he volunteered.

So he did. He considered it "his part" in missions. He gathered the eggs, his mother sold them, and then "they" gave to the mission project. Both the mother and the boy were functioning in helps. And do you think that little boy ever forgot his service to the kingdom that had begun when he was a small child? I asked him about it the other day.

He smiled and said, "I never forgot. . . . That is where I first learned that my part counted, and that if I didn't do my part, then someone else couldn't do his. In fact, sometimes, even today, I use that story as an illustration.

"For if I hadn't gathered the eggs, my mother wouldn't have had the eggs to sell to raise the egg money for the mission. And if the money hadn't been sent to the mission in Bolivia, the missionaries couldn't have kept the school open. And if the school was no longer there, the nationals wouldn't have had any place to learn about Jesus.

"If the nationals hadn't learned about Jesus, there would have been no one to tell the warring tribes in the forest that they could live in peace. And if the tribes hadn't learned to live in peace, there would have been thousands who died without ever hearing about Jesus.

"All because I hadn't gathered the eggs for my mother to sell so she could use the money to send to that mission school in Bolivia." He grinned. "No . . . I could never forget when, where, and how I first learned to function in helps."

She was just a little woman who lived across the street. She was a widow on a very limited income, somewhat crippled, which made it difficult for her to walk to town to buy her groceries. So she asked her neighbor boy to run errands for her. The nickel she gave him was a pittance compared to the time he spent. But he said, "It doesn't matter, because I want to be like my daddy. And my daddy does things for Jesus' sake."

Do you know of persons, young or old, who spend time reading books and the Bible to a partially blind person? I do. In fact, I know of several who do. They're all from the same family. Each member of the family goes to "Pinky's" house one day a week. Mary, whose personal gift is administration, searches the papers and magazines for interesting, upbeat stories of world happenings to read. The father, whose personal gift is mercy, reads the Psalms to Pinky, five of them each day—"So I can saturate her with God's loving kindness."

Millie, whose personal gift is giving, saves her allowance in order to buy the newest Christian books to read to Pinky. The mother, whose personal gift is ministry, reads books and magazine articles written especially for the blind that will help her to become more self-reliant.

And Meron, whose personal gift is prophecy, has set up a very ambitious reading schedule for himself: "I am reading the Bible through to her this year," he said. "Because it's only the Word of God that sets people free."

Do you have small children in your home? Do the older siblings care for the younger? Do they do it as unto the Lord—because that's the way you do it?

Do you help your neighbors repair their plumbing or paint their house—as unto the Lord? Do you bake for "Old Mr. Jones, who is all alone," and spend time sharing yourself and the Word with him? Do your children see their parents serving the Lord and the Lord's people? Is your family enlisted in the growing army of volunteers (some salaried, some not) that is seeking ways to "share in the labor" of the function of helps?

You can be certain that your children are watching you. And if you "magnify your office" (Romans 11:13), as the Apostle Paul did—then so will your children.

Show them the charts in this book, or draw your own charts appropriate for their age; but tell them both by word and deed that *each one* of us is necessary *to* the Body and that God has given *each one* of us an important place *in* the Body.

It doesn't matter what one's personal gift is (which determines the "approach" he takes to whatever service he performs).

Everyone is needed in the function of helps. In the final pages of this chapter, I am giving two excellent suggestions which any family can use (regardless of ages), which will enable any person, child or adult, to become involved in the function of helps.

The first suggests how you, and each individual in your family, can become a World Prayer Missionary. In my last book, *The Idea Book for Mothers,* I spoke about the use of maps to help guide your children into becoming men and women of God who would serve the Lord with a world-wide perspective. Maps: world maps, country maps, U.S. maps, state maps, street maps, neighborhood maps, Bible maps, Israel's wanderings maps, Israel's tribes maps, Kingdom of Israel maps, Travels of Jesus maps, Missionary Journeys of Paul maps.

I taped maps to the walls in our kitchen. And anytime a "place" was mentioned in a conversation, we'd all find the proper map and locate the spot under discussion.

In addition to the maps, which encouraged and fostered the children's "world concept," I invited visiting missionaries to come and partake of a meal, or to spend the night. I asked them to share their world with us, which they gladly did. I invited foreign exchange students to stay with us for varying lengths of time. Then I sent each of the children to travel in some of those countries we had discussed and visualized.

All of this was good and played an important part in helping each of my children to gain that "world vision." The vision is already manifesting in numerous ways, as each person reaches out from his personal approach in the function to which he has been called and begins doing his part in sharing Jesus with the world.

Terry has gone to Japan and Africa for this express purpose. Keith is preparing to leave for the Middle East, where he will be responsible for helping make arrangements for the 1984 Middle East Christian Leader's Conference.

However, I was recently exposed to a new, God-given plan for World Missions that far exceeds anything I knew to do while my children were growing up. It came about when I went to a seminar at the church we attend in Van Nuys, California. The name of the seminar was, "How to Be a World Prayer Missionary." It's a plan that can be utilized by any person or any family.

The concept teaches each "World Prayer Missionary" how to personally and individually select a country of the world, then a region within that country, and finally a base city within that region. You will begin to think and move as though you were actually there.

If you choose: Calcutta, India—You will begin to pray for the sad plight of whole families living on a six-foot square of sidewalk, exposed to the public and the weather.

If you choose: Medan, Sumatra—On behalf of the Christian workers, you will resist Satan's attacks as he constantly barrages the people with demonology and white witchcraft.

If you choose: Bogotá, Colombia—Emerald capital of the world, with streets jammed with international merchants, you will pray that people's vision be changed from seeking the world's treasures to "seeking first the kingdom of God."

As you involve yourself in this world prayer ministry, you will be fulfilling Jesus' command to "Pray ye therefore" (Matthew 9), and "Go ye therefore" (Matthew 28). And as the Rev. Dick Eastman (founder and president of the "World Prayer Missionary" plan) said so well, "Unless there is a 'pray ye therefore,' there will be no 'go ye therefore.' "

This program assists you in learning to pray "creatively." As you involve yourselves in the program, you and your children will learn how to develop and use "Strategy Prayer Cards" which will enable you to pray systematically as well as creatively. Even the preschool child can make his own cards (with your help, of course), utilizing drawings and clipped pictures from magazines instead of words.

When each of us gets hold of the truth that "something happens when I pray that does not happen when I don't," we will realize, "If I haven't prayed today, something has gone undone in God's kingdom." Then a new understanding of the vitalness of "my part" in the Body of Christ and a new excitement will sweep through the church, as together we blanket the earth with the freeing news of salvation.

So I encourage each one of you to join my family and thousands of others in this exciting new avenue for sharing Jesus with the world. For further information and your own packet of starter materials, contact Dick Eastman, Executive Director of Change the World Ministries, P. O. Box 5838, Mission Hills, CA 91345.

Another idea I want to share with you is a way in which you can individually, physically serve the Body of Christ. It's a way which Jesus not only speaks of, but shows us how to accomplish. He spoke of and demonstrated this function of helps in John 13. There, at the close of the Passover meal and at the founding of the institution we call the Lord's Supper, Jesus girded himself with a towel, took a basin, and washed his disciples' feet.

When some of them objected, Jesus said, "Unless I wash you, you have no part with me. . . ."

Then all of them, including the recalcitrant Peter, acquiesced. When Jesus had washed their feet, he sat down and explained to them what this was all about. "You call Me Teacher (Master) and the Lord," he said, "and you are right in doing so, for that is what I am.

"If I then, your Lord and Teacher (Master), have washed your feet, you ought—it is your duty, you are under obligation, you owe it—to wash one another's feet (John 13:13, 14, *The Amplified Bible*).

I am not for a moment trying to tell you that you must now institute foot-washing in your church, fellowship, or denomination as a sacrament, or even as a regular practice. But what I am saying is, I believe, of even greater individual importance than that. For our family has found joy in the humble practice of massaging another person's feet.

First of all, a foot massage brings untold physical and emotional benefit. If you don't believe that, ask a member of your family to rub your feet. And if such a simple massage is beneficial from an "untaught masseur," imagine how much more so a foot massage would be from a "taught" masseur.

A foot massage can quiet a colicky baby, help drain stuffy and achy sinus cavities, renew late-in-the-day energy levels to morning freshness, relieve coughing spasms, and send a fresh surge of energizing blood flowing throughout your body, relaxing tired, tense muscles. These are just starters.

But above all, a foot massage can soften the resistance of a nonbeliever to become receptive to hear the Word of God. Such as the time when Lou invited Bob and me over to share the love of Jesus with her and her husband. But Bruce not only didn't want to talk about God and his Word, he didn't want to hear about it either.

During the course of the evening, Bob noticed that Bruce was having some evident difficulties with his back. Bob said, "Let me give you a foot massage. I believe it will help you."

Bruce looked dubious. But Bob gently persisted, and because of the pain he was suffering, Bruce finally sat down and took off his shoes and socks. After a few minutes of massaging, a look of incredulity swept over Bruce's face.

"This is crazy!" he said. "You rub my feet and my back feels better. . . ."

But as Bob continued in his labor of love, Bruce rather timidly asked, "You were saying that God has a plan for every person's life? Do you really mean that? Even for me?"

So God used a man on his knees, who in humility and love had taken another man's feet in his hands, to bring forth a new creature in Christ.

We have seen it happen again and again. We massage someone's feet and this physical contact opens the door for reaching that person's innermost being. For somehow the intimacy that results from handling another person's feet does not come about with any other physical touching.

Might not this have been what Jesus was referring to when he said, "You are under obligation . . . to wash [handle] one another's feet"?

Foot massages are a way of life at our house. This is a service that all can participate in and all can benefit from. And as each of our children have benefited from them, we send them forth in a spirit of humility to serve others in the way they have themselves been served.

Now you can tell all those "little Davids" on the front row of their play-churches that they "can be somebody now," and then you can lead the way in showing them how.

FOURTEEN

LEADING YOUR CHILD IN PRAISE

All of Jerusalem is astir this feast day. The city is crowded with worshipers from miles around. But a special excitement is evident to those who are crowding into the Temple area.

"Did you see him?" one bearded rabbi asks another.

"See him? Did I see whom?"

"Him! The Messiah. . . . He came to. . . ."

"The Messiah? What do you mean? He came . . . where . . . when?"

"He came into the city today."

"Today? The Messiah?" He lifted his eyes heavenward. "Blessed be his name!" He gripped the first rabbi's arm. "And did you see him yourself?"

"Yes. Blessed be he. I saw him. All the people saw him. And they were praising him. They were shouting, *'Baruch ha-ba*. Blessed is the coming One. Hallelujah! Hosanna to the Son of David!' "

"They said that?"

"Yes, and they threw down palm branches before him."

"Palm branches for the Messiah?"

"Yes . . . and for his donkey. . . ."

"His donkey? Donkey?" The second rabbi laughed loudly. "The Messiah, he rides a donkey?" By this time others joined the little group. They laughed also.

"The Messiah . . . riding a donkey? You must be full of new wine!"

Their conversation was interrupted by angry shouts. "What are you doing? You can't do that!"

"Stop him. Get the Temple police!"

The conversing men turned. Suddenly the first rabbi shouted, "Look—there he is! It's the Messiah! Blessed be he."

As they watched, a tall, bearded man grabbed the edge of one of the moneychanger's tables, and with one heave of his powerful shoulders, the table and its contents went down with a crash. Above the rabble shouts *his* voice could be heard.

"You have made my Father's house a den of thieves! Take your money and get out!" he was saying. A whip in his hand rose and fell. The merchants and their customers scattered.

In the sudden stillness, a thin, plaintive voice shrilled above the crowd. "Rabbi . . . Rabbi . . . have mercy on me! Have mercy on me."

The blind beggar tapped his uncertain way in the direction of the cause of all the commotion. The Man stopped. As the blind man tapped his way closer, a soft smile came to the Man's face. He reached out and touched the blind beggar. "Be healed," he said softly. "Receive your sight."

The blind man dropped his cane. "I can see! I can see! O, thank you, Rabbi."

Within moments, the Man was surrounded by the crippled, the blind, the hopeless ones. And he paused, ministering to each one.

"Hosanna! Blessed is he that cometh in the name of the Lord!"

The Man looked up. Then he saw the children. Scores of

them. Their faces aglow, hands upraised. "Hallelujah . . . Hosanna . . . to the Son of David. . . !"

They stood apart, their eyes upon Jesus. Shouting, singing praises.

The chief priests and scribes saw the children too. They looked first at the children, then at Jesus. Anger convulsed their faces. They crowded around Jesus.

"Don't you hear what they are saying?" the spokesman asked. "They are praising you . . . they are calling you the Son of David. The Messiah. . . ."

Jesus calmly turned to them. "Yes, I hear them," he said. He shook his head sadly. "And haven't you, the leaders of Israel read, 'Out of the mouths of babes and nursing infants you have perfected praise'?"

Then Jesus turned and smiled at the children.

Jesus was quoting this truth from Psalm 8. And what was true in Jesus' day is still true: Perfect praise comes from the lips of children. In the above story, paraphrased from Matthew 21, these children had learned how to praise.

They had seen their parents praising Jesus as he rode into Jerusalem. These children were modeling themselves after their parents, following their example.

In today's culture, many of us have never seen this type of public demonstration of praise. In fact, few of us have anything but a rather hazy idea of the nature of praise, or of its importance. Since we little understand the dynamic of praise, we neither praise effectively, nor teach our children to praise.

At this point you may be thinking, "Wait a minute, I thought this book was about styles of parenting and now I'm suddenly reading about praise." Let me explain: These final four chapters are what I believe to be vital elements in parenting, regardless of what your personal gift or function may be. They deal with a "way of life" one must walk in, in order to move in the fullness of the joy, service, and power that are available to us.

So what is this power-source of praise? How do I tap into it? Let's first listen to David, the psalmist, who said, "I will bless the

Lord at all times; his praise shall continually be in my mouth" (Psalm 34:1).

The writer to the Hebrews said, "By him therefore let us offer the sacrifice of praise to God continually, that is, the fruit of our lips giving thanks to his name" (Hebrews 13:15).

In these verses we see that praise is directly correlated to the words of our mouth. But in teaching our children to praise, what words are we to teach them to say? The words of God. And for this, the best place to begin is by singing Scripture. To assist you in this "praise adventure," there are numerous Scripture song-books, Scripture tapes and records on the market. One I especially like is the "Scripture Sings" songbook. (If your Christian bookstore does not stock a "Scripture Sings," one can be ordered along with singalong cassette tapes from New Life Publications, Inc., 143 Tuxedo Drive, Thomasville, GA 31792.)

By saturating your home with singing Scriptures, you will find yourself, along with your children, blessing the Lord at all times, and his praise will continually be in your mouth.

Listen with me to the words of Vep, a Bible school teacher, who was teaching his students how to sing praises.

Vep said, "Let's begin our praise with Psalm 3:3, 'Thou O Lord art . . . the lifter up of mine head.' You can't praise God with your head hanging in embarrassment. So lift your heads up!

"Now that your heads are up, lift up holy hands. Lift up your hands to the Lord (Psalms 63:4; 134:2; 141:2; 1 Timothy 2:8). Lift them up all the way. Notice how your diaphragm is able to function correctly when you do.

"And now, 'Open thy mouth wide, and I will fill it,' says the Lord" (Psalm 81:10).

"Part of the reason some people are unable to sing praises unto the Lord in a wholehearted manner," Vep says, "is because they have failed to follow these instructions God has given us."

The Psalms lend themselves especially well to being sung, for they are poems whose form is music and whose substance is praise.

LEADING YOUR CHILD IN PRAISE

The Scriptures are living. They are God's living words. To live is to breathe, to move, to feel. Our singing of the Psalms should help us feel them so deeply that we must respond: by lifting our heads, our hands, our voices.

If you have very young children, teach them action choruses with simple movements that clarify the words of the song, such as:

> *Only a boy named David,*
> *Only a little sling,*
> *Only a boy named David,*
> *But he could pray and sing . . .*

But don't limit this physical involvement with your singing to just young children. Move to more complex choruses and Scripture verses using simple motions to bring out the meaning of the words. Let the focus of this action singing be to praise God.

This should be very natural, and will be, once we completely understand the meanings of some of the English and Hebrew words we use as praise words. For example, some of our English synonyms for the word "praise" are "to extol" (meaning to lift up), "exalt" (meaning to raise high), and so on. Remember: Jesus said, "If I be lifted up, I will draw all men unto me." And when we as parents lift up Jesus in our praise, he will draw our children unto himself.

It is essential for children to both see and hear their parents praising God—irrespective of their circumstances, and whatever the setting. Children model after their parents. We teach them both by our words and our examples.

In his book, *The Celebration of Discipline,* Richard J. Foster says, "We are to present our bodies to God in worship in a posture consistent with the inner spirit in worship. Standing, clapping, dancing, lifting the hands, lifting the head, are all postures consistent with the spirit of praise. To sit still, looking dour, is clearly inappropriate for praise."

A careful perusal of praise in the Psalms alone makes it clear that God desires us to praise him with our whole being. "To prostrate" is oftimes a more literal translation of the Hebrew words of praise than the more familiar "worship"; and "to kneel" is more literal than "bless." And when you see the word "thanksgiving," it is often actually referring to the physical act of "extending the hand."

There are many clearly described positions of worship and praise mentioned in the Scriptures, such as: kneeling, lifting the hands, clapping the hands, lifting the head, bowing the head, lying prostrate, and dancing.

The scriptural concept of praise is that it involves more than the thoughts of one's mind and the words of one's mouth. Praise is also physical. We are to offer to God our bodies—in fact, the totality of our beings.

"Often our 'reserved temperament,' " Richard Foster says, "is little more than fear of what others will think of us, or perhaps unwillingness to humble ourselves before God and others."

After having studied chapters 2 and 8, and having learned your personal gift, you might even use the distinctive traits of your gift as a reason for holding back, for not wanting to become physically-involved in your praise to God. For example, you might say, "people with my personal gift are not emotional . . . or with my gift they are more logical . . . or more something else. Or whatever. . . ."

I used to do that. I felt uncomfortable in becoming physically involved in a "worship" service, doing things like clapping my hands. It didn't seem to me to be "worshipful." And I certainly didn't want to raise my hands; that seemed so, well, "unsophisticated."

I thought for years that I felt this way because of my personal gift (which seemed so "intrinsically" me). "Getting physically involved doesn't meet my need," I said.

But I have come to understand that most of our inhibitions are learned, that they have been taught to us and have become a part of us since childhood. We have conformed to society's (or more accurately, our individual environment's) definition of what is "proper and fitting" and what is not, in many things—including how to praise God.

Not until God spoke to me about my attitude did this begin to change for me. But one day I knew he was saying, "Your praise is not to be given for the purpose of meeting 'your need,' but it is to be a sweet-smelling sacrifice unto me."

And all of us know that God never commands us to do something that we cannot do. So I began the process of learning ways to make my praise a sweet-smelling sacrifice unto him.

If I were to say to one of my children, "Kiss your grandmother," and he replied, "I do kiss my grandmother," but there was no overt behavior in response to my command (even though he was capable of it), then the child would not be obeying my command. *Not to physically respond* to a clear command is to fall short of the expressed intention of the command.

God commands us to praise him. And if my only response to his command is to say, " I do praise the Lord," then I am falling short of both the overt expression and the intent of God's command. The reason: The intent of his command is for me to praise him with my whole being.

Praise's origin is in the spirit, through the mind, but praise will manifest itself in both the mouth and the body of the praiser.

One of the ways I can teach my children to manifest their praise in his temple (their bodies) is in dancing. "Let them praise His name in the dance," reads Psalm 149:3, 4. "Let them sing praises unto Him with the timbrel and harp. For the Lord taketh pleasure in His people."

A year ago my family and I were invited to a Jewish celebration of Hannukah in Los Angeles. It was a joyous occasion. Since we were about the only non-Jews present, our eyes and ears were totally open to all that was going on around us.

To us, one of the most moving, most expressive gifts of worship to God we had ever witnessed took place that night when a Jewish family shared a time of worship with us. The father and mother played their Hebrew instruments while their three young daughters danced before the Lord. We were aware of the sacredness of the moment, which epitomized Jeremiah 31:12: "Then shall the maidens rejoice in the dance. . . ."

Their fully-clothed bodies expressed in a lovely, nonsensual way, their adoration of God. Their eyes, their faces were aglow with vibrant life as they offered themselves to the Almighty.

Seldom have I been as moved as when I witnessed total worship: in word, facial expression, and a "lifting up, a reaching up to, an abandonment to God." This, I believe, is a form of praise that God delights in.

As a Jew himself, Jesus would have seen the dance as a natural, integral part of life. There are many biblical examples that illustrate this fact. Throughout the Old Testament it is clear that to the Israelites, dance was as natural a vehicle through which to offer praise to God as was the voice, lifting up praise and thanksgiving.

After the triumphant Exodus from Egypt, and the Children of Israel were finally freed from their bondage of 430 years, Moses and the Israelites sang this song to the Lord, saying, "I will sing to the Lord, for he hath triumphed gloriously: the horse and his rider hath he thrown into the sea" (Exodus 15:1).

Notice the worship after and even during the singing. "And Miriam the prophetess, the sister of Aaron, took a timbrel in her hand; and all the women went out after her with timbrels and with dances" (Exodus 15:20).

And when the Ark of the Covenant was finally brought back into Jerusalem, "David danced before the Lord with all his might" (2 Samuel 6:14).

You can see that the praise of God in the dance is a visual expression of the totality of life. Such physical movement in worshipful praise can communicate directly to our hearts something of the reality of God's Spirit in and among us.

This expression of the entire being reaching out and up to God can sometimes encourage us to receive or recognize things in ourselves that mere words have failed to touch.

My friend, Catherine, who is part of a growing movement learning to praise the Lord in dance says, "Our bodies are the temples of the Holy Spirit, and we are to offer them up to God completely, committing them to him, acknowledging his creation and our sacrifice.

"As your children discover the wind, animals, plants, all of God's natural world that makes up our ambience, encourage them to imitate the movement of the wind, the willowy swaying of the flowers and trees. Explain how God created these things for our enjoyment and to be a part of our lives. Then give thanks together with them for the Father who created all this for us to enjoy and to serve a purpose in our lives.

"The Psalms tell us to sing with a loud voice before the Lord, playing skillfully on the instruments, and to dance before the Lord. In addition to praising God, dance and movement is important for the building up of the body's muscles. But with the dance, we are to express the attitude that our bodies were created to be the temple of the Spirit and to be used to express our love and thankfulness by glorifying God."

All of Catherine's sentiments are dignified by *The Interpreter's Dictionary of the Bible*'s definition of dance, as "the harmonious and rhythmic movement of the body in sheer exuberance of spirit and bodily health, in practical mime, or in conscious devoted joy before God."

The Hebrew words for "dance" in the Old Testament reflect the joy and energy of the dance used in everyday life and on religious occasions. A partial list of them is as follows:

sohek—to play (Jeremiah 31:4)
raqad—to leap, skip (like a child) (1 Chronicles 15:29)
hul—to whirl (Judges 21:21)
pizez—to leap, show agility (2 Samuel 6:16)
hazan—to keep festival (1 Samuel 30:16)
mehulah—choral dance (Judges 11:34)
karar—to dance, move around (2 Samuel 6:14)

Children are very responsive to praising with dancing. We were recently reminded of just how natural it is to worship God with our whole bodies, with all our faculties. My daughters were baby-sitting for Alwyn. As Alice played the piano and Trish sang to her, Alwyn responded spontaneously.

The song the girls sang and played was, "Running over, running over, my cup is full and running over. Since the Lord saved me, I'm as happy as can be. My cup is full and running over." Alwyn immediately responded. She smiled happily and clapped her hands with Trish. And, in addition, she began to dance around. She did it naturally, with no inhibitions or holding back. This demonstration was, to us, a valuable object lesson of natural, spontaneous praise.

Tiny children will always respond to uplifting music. They will sing, lift their hands, move their feet, shout, and clap with great joy. Without any overt encouragement (but, lacking discouragement) they will respond to the music with the totality of their entire being. Young children will automatically do this until they learn from their models not to praise God in this way. But if they are discouraged from praising God with this gift of praise and worship to him, then the proper use of this faculty will be perverted.

Satan was the first to pervert this gift God had given him. In Ezekiel 28:13 we are told that Satan was "filled with music" in the day he was created. Perhaps it was because Satan had personal knowledge of the intrinsic power music possessed, that could involve the total being in praise and worship, that he has perverted its use through egocentricity, aggressiveness, and eroticism. But since music was created in heaven and given to God's children as a means of praise and worship, we must not allow Satan's perversions to prevent us from using music, singing, and dancing as instruments of giving glory to God.

And the only way music will be given its intended place in our praise is for parents to lead their children in singing and dancing before the Lord.

The biblical concept of praise does not fit into our stereotypical times of silence. All of the Hebrew terms for praise have "built into" them something of a public, vocal nature. In the

Hebrew context, praise occurs when you tell somebody about the goodness, the grace, the power, the love of God. And you cannot do that inauspiciously or silently.

Let me, for example, define a few of the Hebrew words that have been translated into English as "praise" words. One of these is *halal*, which is the word that is written "Hallelujah!" in the English. It means, literally, "Praise the Lord!" Or, even more literally, "Praise Yah!" ("Yah" is the abbreviated form of one of God's names: "Yahweh.")

Halal means "to be excited in joy," or "excited boasting." When we realize what our God has done—and what he is yet doing for us, it certainly occasions "excited boasting."

Everyone loves to boast, especially children. Can you remember small boys boasting about which of their fathers is "the greatest"? Here is your opportunity to teach your child how to boast in an acceptable manner: boast about his God.

Have you told them the Bible story about Naaman, who was captain of the host of the king of Syria? It's a good one to remind them (and yourself) of. By way of review, Naaman was a great man. He was an honorable man, a mighty man of valor. But Naaman had a problem. He was a leper. That is, he had leprosy.

Had his leprosy been discovered, he would have lost his position and been banished from society. What should he do? A little girl servant of Naaman's wife provided the answer. She "bragged or boasted" about her God.

She said, "Would God my lord were with the prophet [of God] that is in Samaria! for he would recover him of his leprosy."

The account is given in 2 Kings 5. And because this girl boasted about her God, Naaman did go to the prophet in Samaria. And he was healed. Let's teach our children to boast about the exploits of their God.

And then there's the word *zamar*, such as is used in Psalm 92:1, which renders the idea, "to make music in praise to God." The same idea is expressed in many of the Psalms. Look at Psalm 150. By the time you've read through the six verses, you find yourself involved with a whole orchestra: trumpet, psaltery, harp, timbrel, stringed instruments, organs (flutes), loud cymbals, and high-sounding cymbals.

One mother I know who has the personal gift of ministry began to show her children how to create all kinds of instruments—and to play them—when they were still preschool. (I listed some of this mother's ideas in *The Idea Book for Mothers,* Tyndale House Publishers, 1981, in the chapter, "Home Is a Fun Place to Live.")

This mother and her children would give concerts of praise for their family, friends, and neighbors. They would invite anybody and everybody. What so impressed me about these accomplishments was not so much the fact that each of the children, regardless of his or her personal gift, grew up knowing how to play at least one instrument—but that all of these children knew how to really praise God with music.

Another Hebrew word used in connection with praise is *shir,* meaning "to sing." *Shir* is the word used in Psalm 96:1: "Sing to Yahweh a new song; sing to Yahweh all the earth!" The Lord used this Scripture to speak to at least one of today's gospel song writers. This particular woman's personal gift is teaching. And in her songs she tells, point by point, details of God's greatness, of who he is and what he does, of his creative powers and gifts.

This woman believes that every child can and should create songs about God. So she teaches them how to create these songs. She believes that if parents desire their children to write creative praise songs about their heavenly Father, they must first teach about who he is. And if parents will teach and sing these verities to their children, not only will those children remember them better (notice how many of the Psalms recount who God is and what he has done), but they will then have an example to follow in beginning to sing their own creative stories.

The Hebrew culture encouraged believers to truly "get excited" about God and his reality and his excellent greatness! The Hebrew word *rua* expresses this aspect of worship and praise. It means, "to shout in joy," as in Psalm 100:1: "Make a joyful noise unto the Lord. . . ."

Very vivid in my memory is one Easter Sunrise Service when my oldest son was about fifteen. I was in charge of the service for the teens. I had planned a breakfast, after which we were to have singing and a gospel message. We had invited some young people from the "Adam's Apple" in Fort Wayne, Indiana, to be responsible for this part of the service.

During the singing, which consisted mainly of Scripture set to music (the first time I had ever heard so much Scripture sung), the song leader stopped and said, "Let's give a Jesus cheer!"

Then he shouted, "Give me a J . . . ! Give me an E. . . ." The response among some of the young people was spontaneous, electric. Others looked at me with question marks in their eyes, and I knew that they would be telling their parents. Personally, I was shocked! How blasphemous, I thought.

But the Lord spoke to me very clearly: "Don't criticize another's approach to praise." I have since learned that true praise is much different, and much more all-encompassing than I had previously thought.

"Make a 'joyful noise' unto the Lord. . . ."

Yes, that's what it says. And that's what it means. (By the way, children love to shout and make joyful noises unto the Lord. That sort of shouting makes praising God even more exciting than any ball game.) I had been quick to judge something just because I had "never done it that way before," or seen it done that way before. The Lord has been teaching me that that was not a sufficient basis for judgment, and I really don't know everything there is to know about praising God.

So I've set myself up to be a learner, a disciple; and part of my learning, part of this new discipline in praise is becoming familiar with the Hebrew language and culture.

The Hebrew words I have given you are but a few which are used to denote various connotations and nuances of praise, as well as a variety of approaches to praise. But even this brief sampling shows very clearly that all of these Hebrew "praising words" are words that express sound and movement in some manner.

You can see by this that praise to the Hebrew is understood to be vocal and public, an expression of joyful delight in the living God.

Praise is giving honor to God. And it is a viable principle that neither parental nor juvenile resentments nor anger can flourish with the same tenacity when you and I and our children enter into praise. As we praise, our strength is renewed and we are filled with compassion and joy.

When a parent (or a child) is not praising God, it's a sure indication that he is ailing spiritually. You can tell the spiritual condition of any person or home by his praise—or lack of it.

Praise becomes a deliberate and disciplined adventure for a family that is growing and becoming spiritually mature. And one of the vital spiritual life signs of a healthy Christian family is a responsive attitude toward praise.

Praise is not to be static. It is to be continuous, as stated in Psalm 113:3: "From the rising of the sun unto the going down of the same the Lord's name is to be praised." This principle is crucial to spiritual health and vitality. Praising is not an "if" or "when I feel like it" idea. Verse 2 of this same Psalm says we are to praise the Lord "from this time forth and for evermore."

In order to help you apply the above verses in a practical, meaningful way, I suggest you help your child make a daily "Praise Agreement." The way I do it is to take an 8½″ x 11″ sheet of paper, one for each day of the week, for the entire week. Across the top, print (if your child is able, help him do it himself) "Praise Agreement." Directly below, print *Monday*, etc. At the very bottom of each sheet, draw two lines (one across half of the bottom on one side, the other halfway across the bottom on the other side.) One of these lines is for you to sign. The other line is for your child to sign.

Now, in the center of the page, print a praise verse. Each day of the week (consequently, each page) will have a different verse. If your child is able to print the verse, have him do it. If your child doesn't read, draw descriptive pictures (or clip pictures from magazines and paste them on the page). Post this Praise Agreement in a conspicuous place, where it will be seen several times each day: on the refrigerator, bulletin board, a door to the child's room, or the bathroom mirror. (Note: Use these daily agreements for several weeks, reusing them until each of you has become thoroughly familiar with the praise verses you have selected. Then make new ones.)

Then every morning and evening, and several times in between, call your child's attention to the Praise Agreement, then read it together. This is a beautiful way to memorize Scripture together, but even more importantly, you will detect a new atmosphere in your home, because God has said that he will inhabit the praise of his children (Psalm 22:3). *The Amplified Bible* states it: he "dwells in the holy place where praises are offered."

Personally, I want my home to be a place where God can dwell in the praises that we offer up continually.

Here's another idea that will help fill your home with praise: We hand-print small praise signs and post them in some of the most unexpected places. For example, when you open one of my cupboard doors you will read the sign, "Hallelujah!" When you reach into the medicine cabinet for a toothbrush, you will read, "His praise shall continually be in my mouth." Lift the lid of our piano bench and this sign looks out at you: "And he hath put a new song in my mouth." On the bathroom mirror you will read, "I shall yet praise him, who is the health of my countenance." Inside my closet door—"Bless the Lord, O my soul, thou art very great; thou art clothed with honor and majesty."

Aren't you getting "excited in joy" just reading these great praise ideas? While the excitement is still fresh within you, take time to make your own signs of "excited boasting." You will rejoice as others who enter your home become aware of God's presence and get excited in joy with you.

On the first pages of this chapter we see children praising Jesus and the Father. And we noticed that the devil caused the religious leaders to be more upset about the children praising God than about a crippled man who got healed. You see, God said the praise that comes forth from children will "still the enemy and the avenger" (Psalm 8:2).

For a child who is taught to use his lips to glorify and praise God has been given one of the best weapons available to prevent Satan's encroachment upon his life. Satan knows that, and therefore wants to stop the praises of the children. And one of the best ways to stop the children's praises is to prevent the parents from praising. For then the children will have no models.

So, parents, it is vital that we learn to praise the Lord. And to accomplish this, we must make a commitment.

God has commanded us to praise him. And he has told us that one generation should praise his works to another generation (Psalm 145:4).

So, "Let everything that hath breath, PRAISE THE LORD!"

FIFTEEN

PREPARING YOUR CHILD FOR GOD-GIVEN DREAMS

He was just a little boy. But when his mother brought him to the Temple and left him with the old priest, he didn't cry. He knew why she had brought him. His mother had told him over and over again how special he was to God and how God had *good* plans for his life. He solemnly waved good-bye to his mother when she and his father walked slowly away. Then he turned and took the old priest's hand and walked into the Temple.

And there he lived, because of a promise his mother had made to the Lord.

Though he was little, he followed the old priest around and helped him. The old man told him about God—how God had appeared to Abraham, spoken to him, and blessed him. He told the boy of how Moses had led the Children of Israel out of bondage.

And how God had appeared to Moses on the mountain and spoken to him.

The boy listened and remembered, wondering if God would someday speak to him.

As the priest prepared and offered the sacrifices, the boy watched and learned. And when he was alone he would often pretend that he was the priest and would play that he was burning the incense, or caring for the tables of shewbread, or sprinkling the blood of the animals upon the altar—just as he had seen the priest do.

And all the while, he listened for God to speak to him.

It was night when God finally called him by name. . . .

"Samuel . . ." the Voice came from the darkness.

At first Samuel didn't know it was the voice of the Lord. Eli had to tell him. Then the boy knew. And then he responded. So it was that, for the first time, God communicated with the boy. And because he had been prepared to listen to God's voice, the boy-priest was able to respond to the Word of the Lord.

But what if Samuel had had no one to tell him about how God speaks? And what if the boy had not known how to respond? As it was, though, Samuel had been prepared. Someone had told him. Someone had shown him how to act when God called him by his name.

Samuel's dreaming—his response to God—had been affected by everything he had seen and heard during his waking hours. The same goes for our own dreaming, and that of our children. It is affected by our environment, by the music we listen to, the books we read, the company we keep, the TV we watch. In other words, all of this affects our thinking and our dreaming. And I believe this also includes the dreams and visions we receive from the Lord, either while asleep or awake; they all have a direct correlation to our environment.

Our total ambience affects us: what we are and what we dream. And in Samuel's case, the forces that influenced his life were set in motion even before he was born. Those forces found their genesis in the heart of a woman who prayed.

For many years Hannah had been childless. But throughout all those years she never lost hope. "O Lord," she prayed in the Temple one day, "if you will give me a child, I will lend him to you all the days of his life. . . ."

Hannah received her miracle: she conceived and bore a son. And she named her child Samuel. Hannah loved the child. She cherished him and taught him in the ways of the Lord. Then, when she weaned him, she took the child to the Temple and presented him to the priest.

"For this child I prayed," she told Eli, the priest. "And the Lord has given me my petition . . . therefore I lend him to the Lord. As long as I live he shall be lent to the Lord. . . ."

So it was, that from the very moment of Samuel's birth—and even before—the child lived in an atmosphere that was soaked and surrounded by the things of God and with God's presence. It's no wonder, then, that the child became such a powerful man of God. His influence extended throughout all of Israel and down through the generations to us.

Environments are crucially important to our growth and our children's growth, in every way: physically, emotionally, and spiritually. If you have children now, you can improve their environments by surrounding them with good music (God-honoring, uplifting, inspiring), good books, and especially with God's Word.

If you are expecting a child, you can prepare his environment before he arrives. First of all, you can prepare for him by preparing yourself. Prepare your mind. Prepare your body. Read and listen to the right kinds of literature (in other words, "feed your mind" with good things). Prepare your body by eating good things. There is something else you can do, epitomized by my friend Kathleen:

Kathleen filled her house with praise music. She sang songs of praise to God. She decorated her child's room with soft, pleasing colors and hung God's Word on all the walls. And every day she prayed for her soon-to-be-born child—in the child's room.

Then, after the child was born and came home to dwell in this fully prepared atmosphere, she continually told her little boy that he was special to God, and to his mommie and daddy. She still does that . . . singing God's words to Michael night and day.

Kathleen is committed to fulfill her vow to the Lord, for she had prayed as Samuel's mother had prayed, "When you give me a child, I will lend him to you all the days of his life." Samuel's life and ministry were born out of his mother's godly love and commitment. This will doubtless be true of Kathleen and her son. The same can be true with any mother and with any child.

The Bible, God's Word, is our primary source for ideas of how to live, how to influence our own lives and those of our children. It's not just a book of words, but a real-life drama.

Actually, I've never read a book that more graphically illustrates life stories or tells them so dramatically. This principle characterized Jesus' ministry. He never spoke to a disinterested audience. His hearers always responded to his words, his parables, his unique way of involving them in stories they could relate to, stories that enabled them to see what God was like.

For example, Jesus' story of the Prodigal Son. What better way to illustrate God's forgiveness than this earthly father's enthusiastic response to his son's return home?

"Bring forth the best robe, and put it on him," shouted the happy father, "and put a ring on his hand, and shoes on his feet: And bring hither the fatted calf, and kill it; and let us eat, and be merry: For this my son was dead, and is alive again. . . . And they began to be merry" (Luke 15:22-24).

Could anyone fail to grasp this dramatic portrayal of love, and translate it into a mental perception of what God could do—yea, longed to do for each of the hearers, however lowly his lot?

And the homely illustration comparing his hearers to candles, to light. None could mistake, and none could fail to identify with the analogy. "You—you listeners, you who stand before me right now—*you are the light of the world!* You are important. More than that, you are necessary!"

Then he instructs in how his hearers are to let their lights (their influences) shine forth into a dark world in ways that will bring glory to their Heavenly Father.

We must illustrate God's goodness to our children in like ways. Because if they don't have an understanding of God, of what he is like, and what he desires to do in their own lives, they will be unable to listen to and hear his voice, his dreams, and his visions.

The drama, the conceptualization of God's dreams and visions for us, speaks from the pages of the entire Bible. Take Jeremiah, for example. When God spoke to him, how did he do it? How did he capture the prophet's attention? With something familiar. Listen:

"The Word of the Lord came to me," said Jeremiah, "saying, Jeremiah, what do you see? And I said, I see a branch or shoot of an almond tree [the emblem of alertness and activity, blossoming in late winter]. Then said the Lord to me, You have seen well, for I am alert and active, watching over My word to perform it" (Jeremiah 1:11, 12, *The Amplified Bible*).

Again and again, God spoke to this prophet, oftentimes during the course of his day, using the rather mundane to dramatically drive a truth home. Such as the time when:

"The word which came to Jeremiah from the Lord: Arise and go down to the potter's house, and there I will cause you to hear My words. Then I went down to the potter's house, and behold, he was working at the wheel. And the vessel that he was making of clay was spoiled in the hand of the potter. . . . Then the word of the Lord came to me: . . . Behold, as the clay is in the potter's hand, so are you in My hand, O house of Israel" (Jeremiah 18:1-6, *The Amplified Bible*).

You can see the intense drama, illuminating words, gripping events—all of which influenced those who came in contact with God and his chosen ones. Our children will respond, as did these living Bible characters, when we ourselves respond to God's Word and communicate it to them in relevant ways.

All of us remember what we see and hear much better if it is illustrated for us in a graphic or dramatic manner. But for even better assimilation of that material or information, we need to get involved. We need to *participate*.

Children love participation. Involve them with drama, with mimes. These can evolve from the singing of "action" choruses and from the reading and "acting out" of poetry.

Another excellent way to involve children in "thinking and

dreaming creatively" is to choose stories from the Bible, from lives of Christians (contemporary or historic) and to act them out. To do this you can use simple costumes and props such as can be found around most homes.

In my book *The Idea Book for Mothers* (chapter 9, "Today's Dreams Become Tomorrow's Realities"), I mentioned the "role" chest or "costume" chest we had in our home. This was filled with every imaginable type of "dress-up" clothing: hats, shoes, dresses, shirts, skirts, purses, belts, old curtains, you name it. It was from this rich store of costumes that my children dressed themselves to play church, to give Bible plays, to conceive and act out their own dreams.

The type of activities our children are involved in will be the things they think about. And if these activities are not conducive to the kinds of dreams and visions that bring glory to God, they will be detrimental to the development of this part of the child's spiritual growth.

"Roll your works upon the Lord," reads Proverbs 16:3, "commit and trust them wholly to Him; [He will cause your *thoughts* to become agreeable to His will, and] so shall your plans be established and succeed" *(The Amplified Bible)*.

This is the secret of fostering both the atmosphere and the aptitude in and by which dreams and visions can be conceived, nurtured, and grow.

Let me illustrate: Two young boys who had invited Jesus into their lives at summer camp began taking trumpet lessons at the same time. One family determined to prepare an environment in which their son and brother could prepare for his conception of God's dreams and visions. Here's how they did it:

They purchased tapes and records of Thurlow Spurr, a superb trumpeter, and others of the same caliber. They encouraged their son to listen to them, study them, and learn some of their skills and techniques. They accompanied their son and brother to Christian concerts. They invited friends over for "concerts" and encouraged him to accept any and all opportunities to minister for the Lord.

And they kept telling the young tyro, "You're improving. You're doing well. One day you will minister to hundreds, thousands. . . ."

The young man began to dream as he practiced. He dreamed and he prayed. And his belief in himself grew. He *saw* the scores, the hundreds, the thousands.

And the other family, what did they do? Though they did go to church, they did little else to further the budding young trumpeter's ability to dream. Commendably, they "talked about" the fact that "our son's going to play for the Lord *someday* (when he finally learns how)," but did little else. At home the entire family spent much time each day watching TV and the parents allowed the children to listen to tapes and records of rock music.

Today, the first boy is a minister of music for a large church and is in great demand to play and sing for retreats, conventions, and revival meetings. The second is an alcoholic jazz player.

The godly dreams and visions of the first young man were properly nurtured and thus became a reality. The failure to dream and visualize in a God-honoring way allowed the other young man to drift into the devil's world.

Paul Yonggi Cho was only a youth when he dared to envision himself as one day being the pastor of the largest church in the world. Recently I heard Dr. Cho speak on "Dreams and Visions Are the Language of the Holy Spirit." He enlarged my own "vision" as I heard him tell of the way he had "birthed" the visions he dared to dream.

"God put within me the belief that I should have a church of 100 people," he said. "And at the beginning, when I had no people, that was a lot. But I began to think, to dream, to talk about those 100 people. The seed had been planted. I nurtured, I nourished that seed, until it was ready for delivery. Then the 100-member church became a reality.

"After that, God gave me the vision for a church of 500," he said. "At first this was a phenomenal figure, and I was staggered by it. Then I realized that it was but a seed. I must nurture it and nourish it while it was growing within me. Then, this dream, too, reached its full gestation time and was birthed."

He went on, "This principle is much like that of a pregnant woman. It takes time for the fetus to grow inside her until it is ready for the outside world—till it has reached the size necessary for it to live. If the fetus is aborted it will die.

"Exactly the same principle applies with a dream or a vision that the Holy Spirit plants within a believer. That dream must be nurtured and fed, much like a mother nurtures that little one within her. And if that dream is prematurely 'birthed' or aborted, it, too, will die.

"When you have a dream or a vision within you (and every child of God who is obedient to his Word will be given a dream with which he is to glorify God), then take that dream—feed it, nurture it on God's Word. Speak to it, believe in it. Visualize it as a full-grown 'child.'

"And when the 'birthing' time is ready, it will come forth, literally 'born' of the Spirit of God."

Then Dr. Cho told of how this principle brought to "birth" his church in Seoul, Korea, that has a membership of nearly 300,000 and is growing at the rate of 10,000 new members *each month*.

Daniel was only a child (Daniel 1:3, 4) when his influence was first felt by Nebuchadnezzar, king of Babylon. And from that day until now, Daniel's visions from God have influenced the world.

As a captive child in Babylon, Daniel was one of 50,000 who were captured and "transplanted" into the heathen Babylonian culture. His early training stood him in good stead. He had been taught to love God and to live for him, whatever the circumstances or consequences.

Now Daniel and his three friends were among those selected by the king for special training. These Hebrew children were to be trained "to stand and serve in the king's palace," and they were to be taught "the literature and language of the Chaldeans" (Daniel 1:4).

PREPARING YOUR CHILD FOR GOD-GIVEN DREAMS

Included in the assignment, these children were to be fed "a daily portion of his (the king's) own rich and dainty food." This was to be their menu for three years; then they were to be ready to stand before the king.

Daniel knew that the king's rich food was not conducive to good health, either physical or mental. He knew that his mind would be negatively affected by what he ate, so, "Daniel purposed in his heart that he would not defile himself with the portion of the king's meat, nor with the wine which he drank . . ." (Daniel 1:8).

Daniel made an important point that needs to be made today: The usual "junk food" diets that many American families consider "normal" produce serious negative effects upon all areas of life. Diet affects the way we function while we are awake. And it affects how we sleep. It also has a deleterious effect upon the thoughts we think—and the dreams we dream.

My husband spent nearly two years researching the ways the foods we eat affect us and how they make us the kind of people we are. He learned that the foods we eat and the beverages we drink have *everything* to do with the way we function, our physical output, and our mental output. And even more importantly, diet can affect our spiritual depth and our spiritual services to God.

In other words, "junk foods" produce "junk bodies." And junk bodies produce junk thinking. For example, who *hasn't* been kept awake for long hours into the night, only to finally drop off into a restless sleep, to dream wild, or disconnected dreams—all because of a heavy, rich dinner or a sugar-filled dessert or high caffeine drinks?

Several thousand years ago, Daniel knew that he could not effectively serve God unless he put only good foods into his body and only God's Word into his mind. Thus, later, when Daniel was given an opportunity to speak boldly before the king of the power of his God, he was able to do so because both his mind and his body were pure.

This opportunity came to Daniel when King Nebuchadnezzar

had a dream that troubled him. And when the king's court was unable to reveal the dream or its interpretation to him, Daniel was called. Daniel considered the command, then he and his three friends (all of them still youths) prayed, asking God to reveal the dream to Daniel.

"Then was the secret revealed unto Daniel in a night vision. Then Daniel blessed the God of heaven. . . . Blessed be the name of God for ever and ever: for wisdom and might are his. . . . He revealeth the deep and secret things" (Daniel 2:19, 20, 22).

The answer came to Daniel in a night vision. A dream.

I believe the answer came to Daniel because he had prepared himself to receive a dream from God.

This chapter began with Samuel hearing God's voice in the night. But, in the telling, I purposely left out an important detail: God called Samuel three times *before Eli realized* who it was that was speaking to Samuel. Not until then did he instruct Samuel how to respond.

Why wasn't Eli as sensitive to the Spirit of God as he should have been? Because of the sin he had allowed to develop and remain in his household. If there is sin in your household, your own ears will be dulled as were Eli's, and you will be unable to hear God's voice as clearly as you should. If such is the case, you may miss an opportunity to help your child respond to the voice of the Lord: because *you weren't prepared to hear.*

This is a very serious thing, for Jesus said, "Whoever causes one of these little ones who believe in and acknowledge and cleave to Me to stumble and sin—that is, who entices him, or hinders him in right conduct or thought—it would be better (more expedient and profitable or advantageous) for him to have a great millstone fastened around his neck and to be sunk in the depth of the sea" (Matthew 18:6, *The Amplified Bible*).

As parents we must prepare ourselves and then prepare our children to dream dreams—God's dreams. "For a dream comes with much business and painful effort" (Ecclesiastes 5:3, *Amplified*).

You might ask yourself, as I have continually asked myself,

how much effort have I made to enable my child to realize that God desires to place his dream into the spirit of every child of his? He "is able to [carry out His purpose and] do superabundantly, far over and above all that we [dare] ask or think—infinitely beyond our highest prayers, desires, thoughts, hopes or dreams" (Ephesians 3:20, *The Amplified Bible*).

SIXTEEN

CHILDREN MUST HAVE A MODEL

Terry, at age one and a half, is sitting and "reading" just as I am. It makes no difference to him that his book has no pictures, just words. He watches every move I make. When I turn a page, he turns a page. When anyone asks him what he is doing, he answers quickly, "*We're* reading. . . ."

David is just a few months old and I am sitting in my rocking chair feeding him. "Big sister" Alice, presently two and a half, is sitting in her rocking chair beside me, "feeding" her doll. When I rock, she rocks. When I burp David, she "burps" her doll. When I sing to David, Alice sings to her doll.

Alice says to me, "*We're* baby-loving. . . ."

American social psychology has made a statement during this century concerning something the Bible has said for many centuries, namely: that children learn by watching others. Or to put it another way: behavior is contagious.

And because this is so, *imitation* (or *modeling*) becomes its own reward. For a child takes on the actions of a model without any visible inducement or compulsion to do so, as I illustrated at the beginning of the chapter.

There are basically two ways in which a parent can influence his child's behavior:

INFLUENCE NUMBER ONE:

By doing something which he has never experienced before, a child can be induced to engage in new patterns of behavior.

For example, if my daughter has never baked a cake, I can show her how and teach her to bake. If my daughter has never gone fishing, I can take her fishing and teach her how to fish.

INFLUENCE NUMBER TWO:

By repeatedly doing something he has previously done, the child can be induced to engage in a particular activity rather than in some other activity.

Whether I model *fishing* or *baking* the more consistently during the years will most likely determine the preferred activity my daughter will choose for herself when she gets older.

You can see that in terms of its long-range impact upon the child's behavior and development, the second of these influences will be greater upon the child than the first.

It is a documented fact that one of a child's strongest desires is to do the things that he sees "bigger people" do. Know this, that your child will imitate your every act, even your every facial expression. He will *play the life he sees,* and he will *learn the life he plays.*

If your child is to grow up into a godly man or woman, then that means his "playing" needs to reflect godly living. But his playing can only reflect godly living if that's the life he sees being lived around him.

It was twenty-some years ago when I used to watch Terry preach several times a week to his younger brothers and sisters. This was no easy task, for his "congregation" could get up and leave him or quit "playing church" at any time. To hold his audience, Terry had to develop messages that would interest each member of the congregation individually. Terry learned how to do just that.

And those skills he began developing by preaching to his "first church" are skills that stand him in good stead today. Now as I watch Terry relate to an audience, which he does individually and personally, whether that audience is one, ten, one hundred, or a thousand, I can't help but remember those "play days" that God used to help him prepare for his life's work.

Play in every culture and subculture is truly a child's preparation for life. And in a child's play he emulates his heroes, visualizing himself in their shoes, profession, or occupation. Eskimo children "play" at hunting seals, walrus, and catching fish, thus preparing themselves for adult life.

We must ask ourselves the question: in my children's "play," what are they preparing themselves for? Is the play they are "imitating" fitting them for godly lives?

A child's playing and role-acting enables him to verbalize and act out the life concepts he sees and hears and to crystalize them into personal experience. In *The Idea Book for Mothers,* chapter 1, "Learning to Learn," I give examples of how to roleplay in the teaching/learning of etiquette.

This is good, in fact, important; but it illustrates only the first influence mentioned earlier in this chapter. To complete Influence Number One and make it viable, every child needs to have Influence Number Two—consistent modeling—operative in his life. Otherwise, Influence Number One will possess little lasting value.

For example: Peggy taught her boys what she considered the proper courtesies to be shown a lady. One was the rather basic act of seating a lady at a table. All of the boys learned how to perform this social nicety, but to them it was a dutiful performance, rather than the "manly" behavior they saw around them.

Throughout his teen years, though, when his mother remarried, Darin had the privilege of living in close proximity with a man who always seated ladies before he seated himself. So, after just a few months of observing this act consistently modeled, Darin began doing naturally what had previously been an occasional act.

Prior to "seeing in action" what Peggy had taught Darin in principle, Darin had *heard* his mother's words and had tried to follow her instructions; but in order for Darin to *really* hear her words and obey the spirit of her teaching, he needed a model.

Children usually observe the actions of a model (preferably a same-sex model) to determine whether certain kinds of behavior are appropriate in a given situation.

Children of warm and caring parents tend to be friendly, outgoing, and low in overt aggression. In this regard, my friends, Dick and Nancy, come to mind. When my children and theirs were all small, the discipline standards I held to were more stringent than theirs. But as their children grew older, I found to my utter amazement that the patterns of behavior their children adopted had little to do with a "verbal" standard. Rather, one by one, they had modeled the godly behavior they saw consistently evidenced in their parents.

Aggressive parents (and other models, such as those the children consistently see on TV) tend to breed aggressive children. Children of altruistic parents tend to be altruistic themselves. Ungodly parents bring forth ungodly children, as the Word of God predicts.

"For I the Lord thy God am a jealous God, visiting the iniquity of the fathers upon the children unto the third and fourth generation of them that hate me" (Exodus 20:5).

This does *not* mean that God has placed a curse on some unborn children. It simply means that the modeling that all parents live out before their children results in self-fulfilling prophecy: children generally become what they see consistently modeled.

As the most dominant models for their children, parents thus become not only the most important potential change agents for their children's behavior, but also the established figures who maintain their principal patterns of activity. And insofar as they fail to expose their children to constructive experiences, these models (parents) prevent their children from realizing their full potential.

The Gaithers have written a beautiful song about children in which they say, "You're a promise, you're a possibility, you're a potentiality . . . you can be anything God wants you to be."

And while that expressed principle certainly is true, I want to remind every parent that he is the qualifier for those words, because: parents are the primary determiners of what their children are to become, or fail to become.

For, as psychologist Irvin Child has noted, ". . . despite the enormous number of behavioral options available to each new-born child, he is led to develop actual behavior which is confined within a much narrower range—the range of what is customary and acceptable according to the standards of his (the newborn child's) group."

It follows, then, that any appreciable, enduring improvement in the child's development will be effected primarily through an appreciable, enduring change in the behavior of the parents.

Recently this principle was graphically illustrated for us in our own home by a young man who lived with us for a time. Jay was a new Christian and enthusiastically began spending many hours a day studying God's Word, making full use of Bob's "theological" library. He began to model Bob and the other men around our house, and thus began to evidence rapid spiritual growth.

However, as the holiday season drew near and Jay began making preparations to go home for a visit, I noticed that he was no longer regularly reading his Bible. In fact, instead of the Bible which he had faithfully studied for several months, he was now assiduously studying the current news magazines.

I asked him about the seemingly sudden change.

He said, "I'm going to see my dad, and I want to be able to talk with him . . . and these are the things he talks about."

I knew that Jay's father had been most pleased for Jay to live in our home, knowing that our primary conversations were centered around God's Word.

But Jay knew that, even though his father wanted *him* to be conversant with the Bible, the majority of his father's conversation concerned other things. So, even though Jay had temporarily modeled Bob, his overwhelming desire to *be like* his father took precedence over all other desires.

A father's role is crucial—especially to his sons.

A study done by E. M. Hetherington revealed that boys from mother-dominant homes gave significantly fewer masculine responses to his testing than did boys from father-dominant homes. Boys from father-dominant homes imitated their fathers more than their mothers; while boys from mother-dominant homes imitated their mothers more than their fathers.

It appears that a dominant mother clearly affects the sex-typing of her son; for boys from mother-dominant homes were apparently reluctant to identify with their passive fathers.

In the *Journal of Personality and Social Psychology,* Hetherington proposes that "adequate masculine identification has occurred by age six and . . . this identification [once it occurs] can be maintained in the absence of the father. But if the father leaves in the first four years before [masculine] identification has been established, long-lasting disruption in sex-typed behaviors may result."

I add this information because of the large number of single-parent homes in our society. Parents should be aware of this absolute need for masculine models. And godly men, and wives and mothers of godly men, I remind you that God's Word says over and over again that we are to care for the fatherless. It is the responsibility of all of us to see that no child in the Body of Christ is without a godly male model.

Donnie and Joab are tragic examples of failure in this regard: on my part, as well as those in my church. Donnie was hardly more than a baby when his father abandoned his family. His mother left the church and moved in with an ungodly man, in open defiance of the biblical principles she knew.

The church pulled its righteous skirts about her and ostracized the family remnant, taking the position that no "good" men or boys (including my own boys) were to befriend Donnie and his two brothers. Tiny Donnie was often left with an invalid grandmother and her ungodly husband.

Today it appears that Donnie has been permanently scarred by these events. For one thing, he doesn't know how to relate to men, and is especially uncomfortable in the presence of godly men.

Joab's story, though different, illustrates the urgent need for a boy to relate to an adult male. Joab was only two years old when his father, Leon, was called to the function of evangelist. As such he held evangelistic crusades throughout Southeast Asia, often being gone from home four or five months at a time.

Joab had three older sisters, so he received plenty of loving attention; but because he lacked a godly male model who was involved in his daily life, Joab grew up believing that TLC (tender, loving care) was a "woman's thing." Joab's father was being obedient to the work that God had called him to do and was thus unable to provide that day-to-day godly male model the boy needed. However, if the men in my church (those called to function in helps) had been obedient to their calling, Joab would not have suffered this lack of consistent loving care by godly men.

Sometimes those of us who are serving in the function of helps are tempted to be critical of the children of parents who are serving in another function. This is wrong. We have not been called to judge our brothers and sisters in the Body of Christ, but, rather, to assist them.

The whole Body is to be "fitly joined together and compacted by that which *every joint* supplieth" (Ephesians 4:16), so that the needs of the total Body (in this particular case, the children of the leaders) are met. Let's be more alert to ways in which we can assist parents (and their children) who have been "set apart" to serve in leadership functions.

Although this chapter is primarily about the necessity and effects of parental modeling, I want to also mention the effects of peer modeling. For parents cannot totally maintain established patterns of behavior unless they determine and control how and with whom their children will spend their time.

If a child is born into a family with siblings, then his peers will, of course, be those siblings. And if the first child exhibits a godly life, it will then be much easier for the others to do the same. Although my five children have pursued very different vocations, the positive example provided by the older siblings has been increasingly effective on the younger.

This is a good example of "each one teaching one." If parents take time to teach the older children proper life attitudes and behaviors, there will be much they won't overtly have to teach the younger ones, for the younger children will model the older.

An example of my teaching of manners and etiquette comes to mind. As a child, I grew up in the South when children always answered the call of an adult with, "Ma'am" or "Sir," and always responded with, "Yes, Ma'am" or "Yes, Sir."

I determined that my own children would learn to respond in the same way. However, when my children were growing up, in the northern state in which we lived, no one, neither children nor adults, used those terms.

So when Terry first began responding to having his name called with a "Huh," I corrected him by asking him to say, "Ma'am" instead. He responded cheerfully, but at first seemed to think it was like saying, "Amen," as though it were merely the agreeable end of a conversation. It took time, many months in fact, before these responses became habitual.

However, I didn't have to overtly teach these responses to the younger children; they modeled from the way Terry spoke.

One of the most comprehensive studies relevant to the concerns that affect educational achievement in the nation's schools was done by James S. Coleman. The data used for the study was obtained from over 600,000 children in grades one through twelve, in 4,000 schools that were selected to be representative of public education in the United States. One of the goals of the study was to determine what aspect of the school environment contributed most to the child's achievement. The most important factor by far, the study determined, was the characteristics of the other children who attended the same school.

By the time David had started high school, he had already changed schools several times in the previous three years, and with each move had dropped further and further behind academically. His reading level was far from adequate for his age level. All of this was further affecting the kinds of friends he made. So I enrolled him in a school that touted strict biblical standards of morality, hoping this would upgrade his choice of peers.

For some children this would have been a wise move. But though David did make friends with some pleasant-appearing boys, their focus was upon skiing and other sports. Academically, David continued his "illiterate" (by his mother's standard) ways.

So I decided I must select another course of action. During David's sophomore year we sent him to a boarding school, where most of the students came from highly educated families, and who were, themselves, academically highly motivated.

At first David was astounded by the "high level" conversations that flowed around him. "I've never heard most of their words," he said, "and half the time I don't even know what they are talking about."

Not wanting to be left out, David set himself to learn. He began to make word lists and carry them around in his pocket, whipping them out and studying them whenever he had a spare moment. "I am going to learn to read as well as the best of them!" he said on one of his home visits.

And he did. Even though the teachers at this school were not necessarily "better" than those in the previous school, and the curriculum was much the same, David began taking "giant steps" academically. The key to his dramatic turnaround was his peers.

Whatever characteristics you want your child to develop, the most powerful and effective means to achieve them is to provide him with models who possess those characteristics. Models can come from many sources besides family and friends. Effective models can be outstanding men and women in the Christian world, or in the professional world. Effective models can be sought in books, music, the arts, television, or movies.

Select and monitor these models carefully, because negative characteristics are as transferable as positive ones. "He that walketh with wise men shall be wise," says Proverbs 13:20, "but a companion of fools shall be destroyed."

Check the music your children are listening to. Research the lives of the artists who produce that music (whether they are godly or otherwise), because the music they produce is a direct reflection of the lives they live. And it "comes through" in the music they create, leaving an indelible stamp upon the listeners.

As parents, when we begin to understand the potential power of the modeling process, we will realize the vital importance of selecting models who demonstrate desirable characteristics and arrange to expose our children to them.

I have a further suggestion in this area, which is to expose your children to godly models who possess *the same personal gift your child has,* especially if your child's gift is different from your own.

Benson, whose personal gift is prophecy, has a son whose personal gift is giving. Sixteen-year-old Randy models his father, who is the significant person in his life. But Benson, wanting to enable Randy to fully develop his own personal gift, decided to help him do so.

He told all this to his friend, Martin (whose personal gift is also giving), who handles the portfolio for a large Christian organization. "I would like to expose my son to you and to your approach," Benson said.

Martin said, "I understand your concern. Of course, I'll be glad to be another model for Randy."

So the two men arranged for Randy to spend some time in Martin's office during the summer.

Laura, a high school English teacher, whose personal gift is exhorting, has a daughter whose gift is ministry. Jackie, age fourteen, came to her mother one day with this request.

"Mother, you know how I love to help people, don't you?"

"Yes, of course."

"Well, Paula has asked me to help her at the Good Samaritan a couple of afternoons a week. May I?"

Laura knew that Paula was somewhat of a modern-day Dorcas. She was a seamstress with the personal gift of ministry who spent all her time making and mending clothing for their church's clothing shop that collected and gave away clothing to the needy.

"Why do you want to help Paula?" Laura asked pleasantly.

"Mother, I know yours and my personal gifts differ," Laura said, "and as much as I love and admire you, I'd like to spend some time with someone else whose gift is ministry."

Laura smiled, "I've been praying for just such an opportunity for you. Of course you can help Paula."

As your children grow old enough to understand the nature of personal gifts (theirs and others), it would be helpful to expose them to models *with other personal gifts not evidenced in your family or close friends*. One way to accomplish this is to arrange for seven spiritually mature persons (each with a different personal gift) to speak to a group of believers about the nature and characteristics of their own personal gift.

Such exposure will help your child develop confidence in his own personal gift approach; but it will not hinder his learning from his parents regarding their own personal gift approach.

For example, all five of my children have learned administrative/organizational skills from observing my personal gift approach to everything I do. But they all have used that learned skill in different ways, which at times has made them more effective than I could have been.

For example, Keith, with his personal gift of mercy, has served in a professional administrative capacity in several positions. He has learned to quickly grasp the "big picture" of a situation, formulate feasible goals, and define bite-size pieces encompassing the total project (each portion of which individuals can get hold of). He can then effectively delegate, involving the maximum number of available individuals in such a way as to bring the project to completion within the best possible time frame.

Now these for him are learned skills, but with these learned skills he is able to exercise his personal gift (innate traits) of great sensitivity to see things from another's viewpoint—an awareness of words and actions that might hurt or offend, as well as the ability to identify with those who may be in distress.

His mercy approach draws people to him like a magnet. So in some situations, many potentially volatile ones, the combination of Keith's personal gift of mercy and his learned skills of administration make him far more efficacious than I could be.

From this personal illustration you can see that it's important to give your children the opportunity to learn the best of what you are, which they can then learn to use from their own personal gift approach.

I believe that all parents want their children to be the best of what they are, and much, much more.

Well, I have a suggestion that will enable your child to be and become that "much, much more. . . ." Here's how:

Take a sheet of paper and write this heading: "The Kind of Person I Want My Child to Be." Then write it all down—everything you truly desire your child to be. Everything! Look at the list. Read it carefully. Now *you personally become* everything you have listed, everything you desire your child to be.

For implicit in helping one's child to develop in any area is the development of oneself in that same area. Children may resent being "told" how to be a certain kind of person, but they will not resent being "shown" how.

"Wait a minute," some of you may be saying, "what if I want my child to become a teacher, or a lawyer, or a . . . ? and I can't become that?"

Look back again at what I said. I suggested you write *what kind* of person you desire your child to be, not the vocation or profession you desire for him. However, factors of parental modeling will enter into choices of a profession. And the children of the parents more often than not follow in their footsteps.

So, though you might not be able to become a lawyer, you *can* study law books by checking them out at your local or community college library. You can become familiar with the concepts and vocabulary that pertain to law, then share them with your child.

You can do something else: In addition to sharing with your child (who has expressed such an interest) the excitement of law, you can expose him to some godly lawyers.

Several times in this book I have mentioned how my oldest son Terry has always loved books, learning, and preaching. Through his early growing-up years I prepped him for college in every way I knew. But when he reached the age of fifteen, I suddenly realized that he wasn't talking about college any longer as though it were a foregone conclusion that he would one day attend. The realization stunned me. But as I sat down and analyzed the situation, I recognized the problem: not one of Terry's immediate family (mother, father, aunts, uncles, grandparents) had earned a college degree. Terry simply had no model!

I decided to remedy the situation. One month later I enrolled in college, and within months college once again became an accepted part of Terry's plan and desire to prepare himself to preach the gospel.

I personally believe that man's basic need for a model is one of the primary reasons that Jesus came to earth to live and walk among men. God had previously sent messengers (prophets, priests, teachers, kings) to tell his people how to live. God had even spelled out in explicit detail how one was to walk and live to please him. But it hadn't been enough.

The people needed a model. They needed someone to show them the way. Someone who would say, "Do what I do. Follow me."

So Jesus, along with everything else he was and is, became our model. . . .

Whatever you want your child to be and become, then you become that. Don't just tell your child, "Be unselfish." You model an unselfish life. Don't just tell your child, "Don't be so cross and moody." You model the joy of the Lord. Don't just tell your child, "Study your history. . . ." You check out books of history from the library and read them. Then enthusiastically share your new-found knowledge with him at the dinner table.

Don't just tell your child, "Drugs will damage your body, and *you* shouldn't be taking them." Take a hard look at your medicine cabinets and kitchen cabinets. Clean out and throw away all harmful or unhealthy items. Then you *model* a body that is treated and honored as the temple of the living God.

If you desire a self-disciplined child, then you model self-restraint and self-denial. Say with the Apostle Paul, "Therefore I always exercise and discipline myself—mortifying my body [deadening my carnal affections, bodily appetites, and worldly desires], endeavoring in all respects—to have a clear (unshaken, blameless) conscience, void of offense toward God and toward men" (Acts 24:16, *The Amplified Bible*).

In chapter 9, I listed two principles (Numbers One and Four) describing a child-parent *situation of respect* in which the child imitates the interesting and seemingly competent actions of his significant parent(s). This modeling produces a desire to conform to or to emulate such a parent (or parents) as a method of furthering one's own competence. As a result, the child develops this kind of dependency: a need for guidance and approval from respected models who are more competent than he is.

In Principles Number Three and Five of the same chapter, I spoke to a child-parent situation *where there is no respect,* but in which the child is dependent upon the ministrations and affections of the significant parent(s). As a result of this type of situation, the child develops this kind of dependency: a tendency to imitate parent(s)—or other caretakers—as a means of eliciting nurturance and approval. In this situation, even though there is a lack of respect, the child will eventually (in spite of himself) identify with the early model(s) and internalize their beliefs, values, and attributes.

Earlier in this chapter I told you Donnie's story. In spite of Donnie's bad feelings toward his mother and his dislike for his grouchy, pessimistic grandfather, today, even as an adult, Donnie exhibits his grandfather's mannerisms and values and his mother's beliefs and attributes!

In the writings of the rabbis it is said: "He who teaches a child is as if he had created it, and whoever teaches his son, also teaches his son's son, and on and on to the end of man's generations."

No wonder it hurts me when I hear a parent say, "I wish the Lord would call me to some *significant* ministry. Here I am, just changing diapers, driving in a car pool, and. . . ."

Parents: God has called you into a *significant* ministry, the same one he called Abraham into—"For I have known (chosen, acknowledged) him [as My own]," God said, "so that he may *teach and command his children and the sons of his house* after him to keep the way of the Lord . . ." (Genesis 18:19, *The Amplified Bible*).

As parents, we cannot avoid being models. Whether we will be strong models, weak models, or even negative models for our children is determined by the degree of obedience we give to God's Word.

"He who heeds instruction and correction is [not only himself] in the way of life, but is a way of life for *[his children]*. . . . And he who neglects or refuses reproof [not only himself] goes astray, but causes to err and is a path toward ruin for *[his children]* . . . (Proverbs 10:17, *The Amplified Bible*).

The snow was several inches deep, so I slipped on my boots when I took out the trash to burn. As I bent to light the match, I heard the snow crunch behind me. As I turned, I heard a confident little voice say, "Here I come. . . ."

I frowned as I saw three-and-a-half-year-old Trish struggling toward me through the snow, carefully matching her steps with mine.

She smiled confidently. "It's all right, 'Muver,' I won't ruin my shoes. I'm wearing your other boots . . . and I'm walking *right where you walk.*"

Turn and look around you, parents.

There's someone in *your* boots . . . walking right where *you* walk.

SEVENTEEN

HOW TO BLESS YOUR CHILDREN

This Jewish Shabbat dinner was a brand new experience for us. We had made friends with Bruce and Tamar—principals of the Hebrew school—when one day Tamar invited us to "Come over one Friday night for a Shabbat dinner." We had accepted, set a date, and now here we were: Bob and David and I.

Everything was in readiness when we arrived. The table was aglow with snowy linen, crystal, and aromatic loaves of special Shabbat *challah*. The Shabbat candles were waiting to be lighted. "We have many questions to ask," Bob said when our host had seated us.

Bruce smiled. "We'll do our best to answer them. Then we'll ask a few of our own. . . ."

They hosted us graciously, explaining every move, every tradition. Our entire time together was a beautiful sharing expression of our mutual love for God and family.

But the thing that intrigued me the most was their explanation of how a Jewish father—who is considered the priest of his home—always blesses his wife and children before the Shabbat meal begins.

For the boys, he lays his hand upon their heads, one at a time, and prays in Hebrew, *"Y'simcha elohim k'efrayim v'chimashe."* ("May God make you as Ephraim and Manasseh." In other words, "May a double portion be given you.")

For the girls he prays, *"Y'simaich elohim k'Sarah, Rivkah, Rachel v'Leah."* ("May God make you as Sarah, Rebecca, Rachel, and Leah.")

I thought, "What a beautiful tradition. But of what value is such a blessing? Is it relevant for us today?" And thus began my research into the whole subject of biblical blessings.

"And God blessed them, saying. . . . And God blessed them, and said. . . . And God blessed (spoke good of) . . ." (Genesis 1:22, 28; 2:3, *The Amplified Bible*).

It was a new thought to me: God blesses with words!

I read on.

"Isaac . . . blessed him, and said. . . . Jacob blessed Joseph and said . . ." (Genesis 27:27; 48:15).

God blesses with words.

God's people bless each other with words.

Words. Words. Words. Blessings come through words, because words are creative. God created everything with words. "And God said, Let there be light: and there was light."

"And God said, Let there be. . . . Let there be. . . . Let there be. . . ."

And there was! God created with words. Words are the most powerful, most creative forces, the most effective tools in the universe.

Then, after all the rest of his creative achievements were established, "God created man. . . ."

But, listen to this: God created man, ". . . in his own image, in the image of God created he him . . ." (Genesis 1:27).

God created man with the same capability of creative thought, and the same capability of creative speaking as himself! Think about that just a moment. How do we do anything? We first think it—then we speak it. "I can . . . I will . . . ." We first create in our minds, with words; then we express those words with our tongues; then we fulfill the fruit of our thoughts and our tongues—by doing. In this we follow God's pattern.

God spoke the worlds into existence. With words.

He maintains the worlds the same way. With words.

"He [Jesus] is the perfect imprint and very image of [God's] nature, upholding and maintaining and guiding and propelling the universe by His mighty word of power" (Hebrews 1:3, *The Amplified Bible*).

Words. With them we build and create. With them we tear down and destroy. With them we express love and appreciation. Words. Words. Words. We can do little without them.

Yesterday my husband and I met a lady in church who had just recently emigrated from Germany. She was a lovely lady and we were drawn to her. But she couldn't speak our language. And we couldn't speak hers. We communicated our love by touching and smiling. We were limited in what we could do together. Why?

Because we could not understand each other's words. Therefore, we could not have a complete oneness in our relationship. It takes words to do that.

Remember what God said when disobedient men were building the city and tower which is now known as Babel. "And the Lord said, Behold, the people is one, and they have all one language; and this they begin to do: and now nothing will be restrained from them, which they have imagined to do" (Genesis 11:6).

Words are the most powerful things in the universe. By them we communicate . . . we create. With words we create ideas—ideas that become books, computers, televisions, rockets, satellites. . . .

With words we speak forth a course of action: going to school, buying a car, giving money to missions, witnessing to our neighbors. . . .

The scriptural principle for this is found throughout the Bible. Proverbs 18:21, for instance: "Death and life are in the power of the tongue." Matthew 12:37 is another, in which Jesus said, "For by thy words thou shalt be justified, and by thy words thou shalt be condemned."

In other words, the words I speak determine my actions and become self-fulfilling prophecies. The words I speak set in motion the forces of death or life. The words I speak curse or bless.

I bless my children with my words—just like the Jewish family I mentioned at the first of this chapter.

The Jewish children I know who come from homes where the blessings of God are spoken over them, regularly and consistently, have an aura of confident assurance about them. They *know* that the Lord is their God. And they *know* what his Word says to them. They also know with a certainty borne out by Scripture that God will never forsake his people.

Someone once asked Kathryn Kuhlman, "Why do you believe that the Bible is God's Word?"

She paused a moment, then replied, "Because of the prophecies he has made to the Jews. And the way that they are being fulfilled one by one with meticulous accuracy."

Observant Jews move with the confidence that this knowledge imparts. Our children (yours and mine) ought also to move with the same blessed assurance. But this will come to our children through the consistent speaking of the words of life to them and over them.

So you see, the blessings of God can become an inheritance your children can expect to reap—when you bless them with God's Word.

The opposite is also true: you and I can also bring curses upon our children *by the words* that we speak to them or about them.

I know a man who has a brilliant mind, whose progress in life was stultified (and nearly destroyed) by the words his father said to him. On many occasions his father said, "How can you be so stupid? You do the dumbest things!"

The little boy didn't like arithmetic and wasn't doing well in the subject in school. Because the father did well in arithmetic and his son, Rob, did not, the father again told him, "You're dumb. You'll never amount to anything in life."

It took many years for the young man to realize that he had an excellent mind, and that the "failure syndrome" his father had communicated to him with his words was a "curse." That father had allowed his tongue to kindle a fire in Rob's life that nearly destroyed him.

James has said it so very well: "So also the tongue is a small thing, but what enormous damage it can do. A great forest can be set on fire by one tiny spark. And the tongue is a flame of fire. It is full of wickedness, and poisons every part of the body. And the tongue is set on fire by hell itself, and can turn our whole lives into a blazing flame of destruction and disaster" (James 3:5, 6, *The Living Bible*).

The only thing that saved Rob's life from total destruction was the tongue of a godly person, a person whose tongue had been committed to speaking only as the Holy Spirit led. This person consistently spoke God's Word about him, and over him, until healing finally came to Rob.

But Rob was one of the fortunate ones. Such healing never comes to some who have been brutalized by destructive words.

Never speak depreciatingly about your children. Never! Never! Never! Don't even do it saying, "I was only joking." You may *think* you have been "joking" or "teasing," but the damage is done nonetheless. Words have the power to cut, tear, smash, and hurt in ways that no physical object can. Have you ever looked up the word "sarcasm"? I did one day and was shocked to learn of the word's derivation and its root meaning.

Sarcasm: from the Greek *sarkasmos, sarkazein,* to tear flesh like dogs, to speak bitterly.

Harsh, bitter, sarcastic words to a child (or to an adult) have the power to hurt deeply, to destroy one's self-concept, to depress.

So make it a principle never to say less about yourself or your child than God does. God says he has made you and your child. God says you are wonderfully complex creations and that his workmanship is marvelous (Psalm 139). God says you are created for his glory (Isaiah 43:7). God says we are joint-heirs with Jesus Christ (Romans 8:17). God says that when we place our trust in him, that he writes our name in the book of life (Revelation 20:12).

From the beginning of time, a person's name was considered to have tremendous significance, and the meaning of a name was the prime consideration for its selection. The name was more than just a word attached to a child or person. It was a whole world of possibilities, a world of ideas and experiences, a world of hopes and aspirations.

The significance which was attributed to the name is often emphasized throughout biblical history by the changes that were made in the names of numerous characters, such as: Abraham (from Abram); Sarah (from Sarai); Israel (from Jacob); Joshua (from Hoshea); Jerubaal (from Gideon). In each case these changes were made to honor or to glorify a person's newly acquired position, or to predict the role the individual would play or attain to in the future. The same was true of names that were chosen for a child before he was born (which expressed hope for the future or a desired condition), such as John (God is gracious or merciful) and Jesus (Jehovah my salvation).

A name is a very accurate gauge of the character of a people. As the culture, character, and background of a people differ, to the same extent will the nature of their names be different. Compare, for example, the Teutonic names employed by the early Germans, Scandinavians, and Anglo-Saxons and it will become evident how totally different they are in nature from names of Jewish origin.

Whereas Teutonic names point to the occupation of their peoples as hunters for birds and animals in the forests, and to their aspirations and accomplishments as warriors, the majority of Jewish names have a more spiritual note about them.

Teutonic names, in the main, express ideas of courage, power, strength and nobility, and often incorporate more than one of these concepts in a name. Jewish names express hope, salvation, mercy, and godliness, with only a sprinkling of these other characteristics.

"Strength" in English names does not possess the same quality as "strength" in Hebrew names. The English name denotes the personal strength of the warrior. The Hebrew name as manifested in Hezekiah, Ezekiel, and the like, implies the strength of God.

In the Hebrew, names having an unaesthetic or undesirable meaning have often been accorded euphemistic treatment. This is in keeping with an ancient Jewish practice dating back to talmudic days termed, *lawshon sageenawhor.* In the Talmud a blind man is characterized in euphemistic language as "one who sees light." So if your son is named Cecil (meaning "blind"), according to the euphemistic treatment, he is to be told that his name means "one who sees light." If your daughter's name is Claudette (meaning "lame"), she is to be told that her name means "swiftness."

All of this leads up to the point that your child's name should be established in his mind as having a positive meaning, so that every time he hears his name, he will think of that meaning. Such comforting, confirming knowledge can change his life. It changed the life of Abraham. Here was a man who had no children, and no immediate prospects of ever having children. But God told him (his name was Abram at that time), "You shall be the father of many nations." Each time Abraham heard this "new name" God had given him, he thought of its meaning. And he became the man his name declared him to be.

This principle also affected the life of my son, David. From the time he was little, I told him over and over again that his name meant, "beloved of God." Then I found a plaque that stated such and hung it in his room.

I continually reminded David that no matter where he was, and no matter how negative his situation seemed to be, that he was God's beloved. And whenever he heard someone call him by name he was to remember that they were calling him, "Beloved of God."

It's an unchanging and unchangeable principle that "Faith cometh by hearing . . ." (Romans 10:17). Faith comes by *hearing what God says about us.*

Faith (in ourselves, or your child in himself) also comes by hearing—the words that you, the parent, say about him.

During the course of a day you will normally use hundreds, perhaps even thousands of words. With them you will make requests, you will inform, inquire, command, or counsel—all of this from your own personal gift approach, in addition to the use of learned delivery techniques. Some of your words will be positive and uplifting; others could be competitive or demeaning.

In the use of all these words, for whatever purposes, consider what you say and how you say it. Words like "stupid, no good, sloppy, lazy, clumsy, dodo" and the like, when or if used on your child, could be sparks that ignite a destructive blaze in his life. And if those words are used frequently upon him, those tiny sparks will become a blazing, consuming inferno that leaves destruction in its wake.

I once had an English teacher who told us to think of words as woodworking tools. Most of those "tools" are sharp, powerful, and require experience, skill, and dexterity for their use. All of those tools are neatly lined up along the shop walls and on the bench, ready to be used.

"The tools in one man's hand," he told us, "will construct a piece of fine furniture that commands admiration and a very high price. The same tools in another man's hand produce unsightly, shoddy work, covered with nicks, gouges, and much wasted lumber."

He asked us, "What makes the difference?"

The answer is obvious.

The craftsman is a patient, careful man, one who has been taught to respect his tools and to use them carefully. The other man is untaught and careless and possesses little respect for the equipment in his hands.

Our words are those tools.

Good tools. But how selectively, how effectively, how carefully do we use them?

These words from the book of Proverbs speak to both of these workmen. Regarding the craftsman: "Pleasant words are as an honeycomb, sweet to the soul, and health to the bones" (Proverbs 16:24).

Regarding the careless worker: "There is [he] that speaketh like the piercings of a sword . . ." (Proverbs 12:18a). The last part of the verse speaks to the craftsman: ". . . the tongue of the wise is health."

Again for the careless man: "The words of a talebearer [or the careless with his words] are like wounds, and they go down into the innermost parts" (Proverbs 26:22).

Read the book of Proverbs. It has much to say to parents (and all others) about words, tongue, lips, mouth. As you read through Proverbs, mark each reference to words, tongue, lips, speaking, mouth. In my seminars I tell parents:

"If you will do this prayerfully before the Lord, asking the Holy Spirit to speak to you about the words you say, I believe both your life and the lives of your children will be changed."

One seminar mother reported to me that when she read Proverbs 10:19, the words seemed to "thunder within my innermost being!" The verse reads, "In the multitude of words there wanteth not sin: but he that refraineth his lips is wise."

She told how she had the habit of talking continuously, never listening. She said the Holy Spirit showed her she was sinning because her words were often negative, often unnecessary. Worse, yet, her continual talking prevented her from hearing, *really* hearing her children.

She said, "I made small posters that read, 'He that refraineth his lips is wise,' and displayed them all over the house. It has had a positive effect on my whole family."

You may be thinking, "But I am careful of the words I select and use. . . ."

But I want to remind you that most of the words that come out of our mouths *are not* "carefully selected." They are words we speak from habit, so automatically, with hardly any awareness of them at all. These are the words Jesus was talking about when he said, "For out of the abundance of the heart the mouth speaketh" (Matthew 12:34).

It's a basic principle that the words that are in us in abundance are the words we allow ourselves to hear, to read, to think about.

That's why God says to each of us, "My son [or daughter], attend to my words; consent and submit to [my words]. Let [my words] not depart from your sight; keep [my words] in the center of your heart. For [my words] are life to those who find [my words], healing and health to all their flesh" (Proverbs 4:20-22, *The Amplified Bible*).

Words. Words. Words. They are a parent's most valuable tool. They are containers that carry either fear or faith to your child; either death or life.

As a parent, I must become so word conscious, so *God's Word* conscious that, regardless of the situation, the words that come out of my mouth will be God's words—words of blessing. The words that come from a child's parent's mouth are the most influential force in that child's life and they determine his perceptions about himself and his world.

And the words you cause to fill your child's spirit (mind) with will be the "abundance" out of which he communicates with his world.

God's Word says we can have what we say (Mark 11:23, 24). So ask yourself, "What am I saying and what am I teaching my child to say?"

On the whole, the Christian world is probably not taking this particular dimension of God's Word seriously enough. But the world of psychology believes it *and uses it.* Let me give you an illustration:

The psychological theories underlying Chinese thought-

HOW TO BLESS YOUR CHILDREN

reform hold that if a person is forced to recite words/thoughts/ ideologies on a regular basis, even though he *does not* believe them, that this repetition will in time cause him to do so. The sound psychological principle is, "No one can for very long believe one thing and say or do another."

In time the resultant dissonance will cause a person to do one of two things: (1) either he will adjust his actions and thoughts to fit the words he has been saying; in other words, come to believe what he has been saying, or, (2) he will suffer a mental and emotional breakdown.

Case in point: Within one generation, under the leadership of Mao Tse-tung, China became a Communist nation—without a war! How was that remarkable feat achieved? Every day every child in every school had to recite quotations from Chairman Mao's *Little Red Book*. Adults went to regular mandatory meetings and recited quotations from the same book.

The people were told, "You don't have to believe what you are saying. But you must conform with the others. Everybody must say the same thing."

And, according to the psychological principle I just quoted, in time the entire nation began to believe in the Communist ideology. They came to believe the *words* they had been saying!

The same principles apply to much of today's popular music. For the most part it is subtly destructive. My youngest son is my source of information regarding the gripping, oppressive power of both the lyrics and the music of the so-called pop rock, rock, or hard rock (sometimes used synonymously with acid rock), and punk rock.

"I believe all of this music is demonic," David says, "and even many Christians are being influenced by this ungodly stuff, mostly without even being aware of it.

"Much of the rock music is associated with drugs," he told me, "but even without the drugs, the music itself, with its hard, metallic sound, its crescendoing volume, its nonsensical, *depressive* lyrics—these all produce anti-establishment attitudes and anti-social behavior.

"For the most part, the *words* of the music 'sing' themselves into people's unconscious, influencing everything they think and everything they do. These words—as well as the words from many other types of music—produce self-pity, fear, and death."

David speaks from a firsthand involvement, an involvement from which God's Word has freed him. For it is only God's words that can produce life, because, ". . . the Word that God speaks is alive and full of power . . ." (Hebrews 4:12, *The Amplified Bible*). Words. Words. Words. They are powerful curses or blessings that produce either destruction and death or creation and life. How we use them makes the difference.

Words are like seeds in that they also produce fruit after their own kind. It's a principle as inviolable as the "Genesis principle"—the principle that governs sowing and reaping. If I continually listen to (or speak) words of fear, I will reap fear. If I continually listen to (and speak) words of peace and joy, love and victory, I will reap that kind of a harvest.

I remember one spring when the children were planting their flower gardens. Keith and Alíce patiently dug little trenches in which they carefully sprinkled the minute zinnia seeds. Handling such tiny seeds was too slow for Trish. So she went to the tray of garden seeds and selected a packet of pumpkin seeds, which "are much easier to plant," and proceeded to plant those seeds in her own flower garden.

When summer came, Keith and Alíce were "harvesting" and enjoying their colorful zinnias. They shared them with the family and with friends and neighbors. But Trish had only a green vine to show for her labors, which wasn't even pretty. However, Trish did learn a valuable lesson about seeds producing after their own kind, even though it was too late that summer.

Throughout this book we've been speaking, though indirectly, of sowing and reaping. And harvesting. By understanding our personal gift and operating in joyful obedience in the function where the Holy Spirit places us in the Body, we will inevitably reap a continuing harvest of good fruit.

And some of this good fruit will be the members of our family. You may be looking at this year's harvest and you may not be happy with it, because in the past you did not sow seeds of life, so the harvest has not produced more abundant life in your household. But don't be discouraged, because every harvest is seasonal. You have to sow again and again in order to reap continuously.

And it's *never too late* to sow good seed and reap a good harvest.

Let me illustrate. Gert was a mature woman, with a grown son. Gert was an alcoholic, who had planted seeds that eventually produced an alcoholic: her son.

One might naturally think it was too late for Gert to do anything about her harvest, for she had continuously sown death seeds. And she had reaped a terrible harvest.

If you call a child "worthless" once it might not affect him very much. At least not obviously. But a seed has been planted which will grow and be harvested one day.

Call a child "worthless" a dozen times, a hundred times, and he will begin to believe that he is, indeed, a worthless child.

Then the psychological principle (borrowed from the Genesis principle of sowing and reaping) of self-fulfilling prophecy comes into play, and the child begins to act in "worthless" ways. He literally becomes "worthless."

But in Gert's case that was not the end of the story, for someone sowed God's Word into this discouraged, lonely, defeated woman's life. And the seed took root. Gert received new life in Jesus: a good harvest from good seed sown.

Gert immediately began to sow good seed— the incorruptible seed of the Word of God—into her son's life.

She began to speak words of life and health to her son. She told him, "God loves you. And so do I." She told him, "God says, 'I have redeemed you, I have called you by name. You are mine.'"

She told him, "God says, 'I can make you into a new creation if you will only let me.'"

She told him those words a dozen times, with seemingly no

change in his outward life. She told him a hundred times. A thousand times. And the harvest of previous sowings came and went. Then one day came another harvest. . . .

The harvest of life-giving words.

If you have planted a poor crop and have reaped a poor harvest, plant again—this time with the good seed of God's Word. Plant it again. And again. And again.

"And let us not be weary in well doing: for in due season *we shall reap* . . ." (Galatians 6:9).

And what a blessed harvest!